THE HIDDEN SECRETS AND STORIES OF DISNEYLAND

MIKE FOX

Cover photo by Tom Bricker

ISBN 10: 0692724729
ISBN-13: 978-0692724729

P - ING - 010117

To my wife, Kristy, and my two children, Brian and Megan. Let's all meet in our dreams by the popcorn cart in the Town Square.

THE HIDDEN SECRETS & STORIES OF DISNEYLAND

Includes Secrets and Photos Not Found in Any Other Disney Books, Articles or Web Sites

- The amazing story of how Walt came to acquire the stately "Capitol of Disneyland" – Published here for the very first time

- The intriguing story about the creation of the builder's plates on the E.P. Ripley and C.K. Holliday steam engines

- The story of how a guest recognized an error with the Disneyland telegraph...and fixed it!

- The first-ever revealed connection between the colorful Mutoscopes of Main Street, U.S.A and a young 12 year-old Walt Disney

- How to ride in your own special V.I.P. seat for two up front with the Disneyland Railroad Engineers

- A fun story from Disney Legend Bob Gurr about Disneyland's very first locomotive

- Where to find a collection of hanging lanterns from Disneyland's opening day in 1955

- Where to find *Ochna serrulata*, also known as the Mickey Mouse Plant

- The fascinating stories of why Walt never built Disneyland's International Street and Liberty Street

- The story of why the Hatbox Ghost was "exorcised" from the Haunted Mansion

- Special stories from Bob Gurr, Michael Broggie, Jeff Baham, Michael Campbell, Steve DeGaetano, Jeff Kober and more

- And many, many more! All arranged as a fun tour throughout the park and complete with photos!

REVIEWS

"Since I was on Disneyland property during construction in late 1954, and the continuing additions over 60 years, I thought I knew a lot about Disneyland. Wrong! While reading The Hidden Secrets & Stories of Disneyland, I was shocked at how much I never knew. Almost every page contained details I had never noticed before. - **Disney Legend Bob Gurr**

"It's hard to teach an old mouse a new trick...but this book provides hours of surprises for the most knowledgeable of Disney Fans – **Peter Whitehead – Walt Disney Hometown Museum**

"Having grown up in the shadows of Walt Disney and Roger Broggie, I was delighted to read this book. Even as a summer season Cast Member while in college in the early 1960s, I discovered secrets about Disneyland unearthed by Mike Fox that were new to me. Well done!" - **Michael Broggie**, Walt Disney historian and founder of The Carolwood Society and Foundation - Dedicated to preserving the personal railroad legacy of Walt Disney.

"There are some secrets in this book you just won't find anywhere else. It's well-researched and well-written, and I definitely recommend adding this volume to your Disney library." - **Steve DeGaetano** - Disneyland Railroad Historian

"You'll love The Hidden Secrets & Stories of Disneyland by Mike Fox." - "I highly recommend it to anyone who enjoys Disneyland." - **ChipandCo.com**

FOLLOW
DISNEY-SECRETS ONLINE

On the Web:
www.Disney-Secrets.com

On Twitter:
@149G22

On Facebook:
www.Facebook.com/Disney-Secrets
(Look for the icon above)

TABLE OF CONTENTS

INTRODUCTION

Disneyland is a grand stage upon which a story of magic, fantasy and enchantment plays out for guests from around the world each and every day. Cast Members perform, attractions entertain, parades delight and fireworks bedazzle as guests young and old watch with wide-eyed wonder and amazement as the story unfolds all around them. But unknown to many, separate and oftentimes whimsical stories play out right alongside the main act, and these stories make up *The Hidden Secrets & Stories of Disneyland.*

With your first visits to Disneyland, it's all about the attractions...as it should be. There are pirate ships to sail, spaceships to ride, characters to meet and a dark haunted mansion to explore. But alongside all of these stories is another magical aspect of Disneyland, one which the Disney Imagineers have purposely created for all to enjoy, but few to discover. That old park bench? It's the very bench Walt Disney sat upon when he first thought of Disneyland. The grand Mark Twain Riverboat? You can actually pilot it yourself on the Rivers of America. Want to sit up front with the Engineers running the E.P. Ripley steam engine of the Disneyland Railroad? All you have to do is ask. *The Hidden Secrets & Stories of Disneyland* is your guide to an exciting new way to experience the magic!

CHAPTER ONE

TOWN SQUARE SECRETS

"You can design and create and build the most wonderful place in the world, but it takes people to make the dream a reality.

\- Walt Disney

LADIES & GENTLEMEN... DISNEYLAND!

Unknown by many, Walt Disney designed the entrance to Disneyland to reveal itself to guests as if they were watching the opening of a Disney movie.

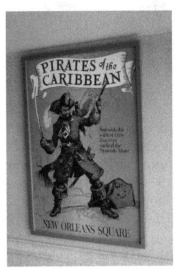

As you pass under the Disneyland Railroad Station you'll notice movie posters on the walls of the tunnels which showcase the coming attractions, including Pirates of the Caribbean, Space Mountain, the Haunted Mansion and more. The smell of fresh-popped popcorn coming from the old-fashioned popcorn cart, *which is always stationed at the entrance*, fills the air as you emerge from the dark entrance tunnels and the curtain rises to the delightful sights, sounds and music of the Town Square. Next, the credits of those who created the movie begin to appear. Colorful and creative, they slowly reveal themselves on the windows of the building facades as you stroll down Main Street, U.S.A. towards Sleeping Beauty Castle. The story of Disneyland then continues as you enter into the different lands and experience the show through a magical day of wonder, fantasy and adventure.

A POP SECRET

So much of Disneyland occurs in the smallest of details, which are easily overlooked. In fact, *millions* of guests walk right past this next secret every year and never notice it.

Stop at the popcorn cart near the entrance to the Town Square and take note of the small character inside turning a barrel of popcorn. Here, as with all of the popcorn carts located in Disneyland, you will find the character coincides with the land in which the cart is located. In this case it is a clown, and perhaps this is a nod to the small clown drawn by Sam McKim found in the large Disneyland souvenir maps issued between 1955 and 1962. Elsewhere guests will find an Abominable Snowman near the Matterhorn, The Rocketeer in Tomorrowland, and an Undertaker at the Haunted Mansion.

"HERE YOU LEAVE TODAY AND ENTER THE WORLD OF YESTERDAY, TOMORROW AND FANTASY"

As with the popcorn cart, many of Disneyland's secrets require guests to stop and observe. Without pausing, they go unnoticed or unappreciated.

Stop for a moment in the Town Square and realize that once you enter the park, you leave behind the "outside" world and immerse yourself in the story that is Disneyland. Walt Disney designed this effect on purpose, encircling the entire park with a high berm of dirt capped with the Disneyland Railroad so that the outside world would not be visible from anywhere within the park.

GET A SPECIAL SEAT FOR TWO ON THE DISNEYLAND RAILROAD

Now make your way up the stairs to the Disneyland Railroad Station where a special seat for two awaits those guests "in the know" about this next Disneyland Secret.

Everyday, thousands and thousands of guests board one of the trains of the Disneyland Railroad and enjoy the Grand Circle Tour around the park. It's a fun way to experience all the sights, sounds and magic of Disneyland from a unique vantage point.

Now be the envy of your family and friends by riding in a special seat for two on the Tender, the car right behind the Engine! Meet the train Engineers, watch as they operate the engine, ask questions and experience Disneyland from a memorable new perspective very few guests get to enjoy. Here's how...

Climb the stairs of the Disneyland Railroad Station in the Town Square and mention to a Conductor you'd like to ride in the Tender. The Conductor will have you stand off to the side as you wait for a train with a Tender seat to arrive. Once it's

at the station, you'll be escorted past the security gate to the front of the Tender where your special seat for two awaits!

Please note: The Tender car is not available until approximately one hour after the park opens, and even then you may need to wait for quite a while. This can be one half-hour to an hour. Be polite and patient when asking if you may ride. Availability is subject to weather conditions and will be declined if it is rainy or too sunny and warm, as temperatures close to the boiler can reach up to 135 degrees on especially hot days.

...'Board!

DISNEYLAND UNDER PRESSURE

One of the reasons the Tender Seat may not be currently available is that the Engineers are performing what is known as a "blow down." Each Disneyland Railroad steam engine has hundreds of gallons of water in it, which is constantly being converted to steam and then exhausted. Tiny particulates within the water don't disperse with the steam, but instead remain and over time sink to form a layer of sediment in the lowest point of the boiler, which is known as the "mud ring." If this mud is allowed to build up, it can cause significant damage to the engine's firebox. To expel the mud, the Engineer opens an air-operated valve in the cab, which releases boiler water with tremendous force, thus clearing the mud ring. Because the boiler itself is a closed pressure vessel, the heated water under pressure inside exists at a temperature much higher than water's normal boiling point, 212 degrees Fahrenheit. (In a boiler operating at a pressure of 150 pounds per square inch, the water is at a temperature of 365 degrees.) When the blow down valve is opened and this heated higher-pressure water hits regular atmospheric pressure, it flashes into steam, roaring from the side of the engine as a loud jet of steam and taking with it any "mud" from the mud ring.

Your Own
V.I.P. Ride Aboard
The Disneyland Railroad

Until recently, Disneyland guests could only marvel at the beautiful Lilly Belle, an elegant red rail car adorned with exquisite Victorian styling reserved only for VIPs. Named after Walt Disney's wife, Lillian, the Lilly Belle would ply the tracks of the Disneyland Railroad with important dignitaries, including Presidents, Heads of State, Disney executives, celebrities and the like, all while guests looked on with curiosity and perhaps a twinge of envy.

Today that's all changed, and guests are free to ride this special VIP car with just a little planning. Stop in at the Main Street Station and mention to a Conductor you'd like to ride aboard the Lilly Belle. You'll be asked to wait for the next

available opportunity, which may not be long. Groups of up to 14 are allowed to ride, and groups with fewer people may find they have the car all to themselves, as few guests are aware of this vintage Disneyland secret. Please note that you must make a full circle tour of Disneyland and the opportunity to ride aboard the Lilly Belle is not always guaranteed, as an additional Conductor must be available to chaperone your group at the time you make your request. In addition, rides on the Lilly Belle may be unavailable during your visit to the park, especially if it is raining hard or the park is extremely crowded.

Note: Check with a Conductor first thing in the morning as to if the Lilly Belle will be available that day.

THE FIRST DISNEYLAND LOCOMOTIVE

Walt was a master at storytelling, be it in the high-flying adventures of Mickey Mouse in *Plane Crazy*, the grand sweeping score of Fantasia, or even the authentic sights and sounds of the Disneyland Railroad.

In July of 1954, construction began on Walt's new Disneyland, and since Walt wanted the park surrounded by a train, work also began on two locomotives which were to be designed and built from the ground up in time to ply the rails on Disneyland's opening day, less than one year away. Here is a story, graciously shared by **Disney Legend Bob Gurr**, which describes some of the work which occurred behind the scenes to place the first Disneyland locomotive on the tracks.

When Roger Broggie set me to work on the Autopia, he gave me a drafting board in a room with some interesting "olde tyme" characters from America's railroad past...steam freaks, I called them. We seemed worlds apart; they were mostly in their 50s to 70s, while I was a green kid of 22. Steam railroads where their passion, sports cars and airplanes were my big thrill. The whole bunch had a leader, Earl Vilmer, a railroad superintendent with over 20 years experience. Real quiet guy, hired by Roger Broggie to head up the whole Disneyland Railroad effort. Another quiet but very funny guy, a model railroader named Eddie Sargeant, was drafting up all the railroad cars. Everyone's favorite animator-steam guru-band leader Ward Kimball was always there to kibbutz. Another combination model railroad guy and story writer was Dick Bagley. Roger had him drafting up the steam engines for the Mark Twain sternwheeler riverboat. But the fellow who took me under his wing and mentored me into the "world of steam" was the pixie-like Ed Lingenfelter. Ed was born back in the 19th century and loved the great monster steam engines as a kid. He learned his engineering trade very early and spent an entire career designing steam locomotives in Pennsylvania. Years after retirement, Ed was hired by Walt to engineer the 5/8 scale Lilly Belle Locomotive.

To get the hang of proper drafting format, Ed had a big chart on his wall explaining the essence of good design communication. He showed me how many ways there were to explain something to a machinist with a blueprint. All the other guys were cranking out tons of locomotive and railroad car drawings. Eddie Sargeant did most of the rolling stock. Earl Vilmer would stop and draw anything needed as well as act as the lead superintendent. Old records show that Earl made drawings starting on December 31, 1954, Sargeant got started on August 14, 1954. Ed started the locomotive erecting diagram on July 30, 1954, but Bagley got going on July 2, 1954. Ed even gave me the headlight reflector to draw up for the Lilly Belle on May 27, 1955.

Ed was amazing; he would draw all the locomotive parts first, get them to the shop, then calculate the design afterwards. Seemed backwards, but he just knew everything about steam by heart. And steam is real tricky when you change scale from full size down to Walt's own Lilly Belle, then back up to 5/8 size. And what a storyteller!

Soon, the first Disneyland locomotive was ready to steam up in the round house. Walt opened the throttle a bit but nothing moved. A bit more and the new locomotive almost silently glided forward. *"No, no, no! Go fix it."*...Walt exclaimed. I was puzzled, so I asked Ed to explain. He chuckled and told me that locomotives have machining clearances expressed as "either tight or loose 1/64^{ths} of an inch." It seems the Studio Machine Shop did a fine job and revised some tolerances to thousandths of an inch. After all, the shop did build precise movie cameras. Ed had warned that his dimensions should apply, so he got a big laugh out of the effort to disassemble the tight parts and open them up. A few days later the locomotive clunked and clanked out of the barn just like a proper locomotive should, using just a tiny bit of throttle. *"Yes."*...said Walt. Naturally, Earl Vilmer and all the steam freaks in attendance smiled and nodded in their conservative silence. To this day, I cherish the knowledge I learned from those wonderful wizards whose world was so far from mine.

WED Locomotive Works

With each completion of the "Grand Circle Tour," the engines of the Disneyland Railroad pull just beyond the station and proceed into a gated restricted area, which allows the passenger cars to come to a stop at the boarding platform. Unfortunately, this means guests never get to see the historical bronze plaques, or "Builder's Plates", which are affixed to the side of the boiler of the engines. In the case of the E.P. Ripley, the plate reads "WED Locomotive Works - W. E. Disney Pres. - R. E. Broggie - Gen. Mgr." 1955.

While each of the engines of the Disneyland Railroad are adorned with a builder's plate, that has not always been the case for two of the engines, the E.P. Ripley and the C.K. Holliday. These engines were built without plates, and they would not receive them until Disneyland's 50th anniversary.

*What follows is an article which explains the history behind these plates, written by **Michael Campbell**, President of the Carolwood Pacific Historical Society, which is dedicated to preserving the personal railroad legacy of Walt Disney. I would like to thank him for graciously allowing me to share his article with the readers of this book.*

Full Plates for Disneyland's Birthday

"Happy 50th birthday, Disneyland Railroad"
By Michael Campbell

The year 2005 marked not only the 50th anniversary of Disneyland, but the 50th "birthday" of two of its steam locomotives: the C. K. Holliday and the E. P. Ripley. These were built by Roger Broggie, Sr. and the machine shop crew at Walt Disney Studios in Burbank, with final assembly taking place at the Park in June, 1955. Although most of the Park was owned by Disneyland, Incorporated, the railroad was Walt Disney's personal property: he paid for the construction of the engines and their consists. The railroad cast members were employees of Walt's personal company, WED Enterprises (later, Retlaw Enterprises).

For unknown reasons, builder's plates were not created for engines 1 and 2 at the time they were built. Builder's plates are, in effect, the locomotive manufacturer's "signature"; they bear not only the builder's name but also the serial or construction number, date and location of manufacture, and sometimes the plant managers' names. They were found on virtually all steam locomotives and are highly prized by collectors. It always seemed odd to me that the Holliday and Ripley should be lacking this common yet vital detail. So, when Michael Broggie challenged the Carolwood Pacific Historical Society to think of unique ways to help celebrate the Railroad's 50th anniversary, it occurred to me that we could "plus" the engines through the creation of custom builder's plates. Michael agreed, so I set about creating some designs to show Disneyland management.

Even though engines 1 and 2 are mechanically identical, great care was taken to ensure that each had a unique appearance. The C. K. Holliday was a reproduction of an 1870's wood-burning freight locomotive whereas the E. P. Ripley was a tribute to an elegant 1890's passenger train. It was important, therefore, to ensure that these plates would fit the individual style and era of each engine. Fortunately, I had the assistance of three of the most knowledgeable and qualified individuals to help determine the best design: Steve DeGaetano, author of "Welcome Aboard the Disneyland Railroad!"; David Fletcher, Master Modeler and railroad archivist from Australia; and, Jim Wilke, railroad historian and consultant to the California State Railroad Museum as well as to major model railroad manufacturers.

After many discussions and the review of dozens of photographs, we decided to fashion the Holliday plate after a Baldwin design of 1872. The Ripley plate, however, would follow the rectangular shape used by Rogers on an 1899 locomotive. Having selected the styles, we came to the much more difficult task of writing the verbiage. These two engines share the distinction of being the only steam locomotives built by WED Enterprises, the private company Walt established to manage the design and construction of Disneyland. (The other engines at the Disneyland and Walt Disney World are re-built Baldwins; the locomotives at the international parks were built by Severns-Lamb and other present-day manufacturers.) I decided to create the fictional "WED Locomotive Works" to take the place of the builder's name as a subtle reference to this fact.

We wanted to use the plates as a way to honor the history of these trains. On the Holliday plate, we included "Retlaw & Co." as the plant managers' names as a way to pay tribute to the fact that the railroad was owned and operated by Retlaw Enterprises from 1965 until 1982. For the Ripley plate, we listed "W. E. Disney, Pres." and "R. E. Broggie, Gen. Mgr." as an honor to the driving forces behind the creation of the locomotives. After careful consideration, we opted to assign the serial numbers "1" and "2" to the engines to signify that they were the first and second locomotives built by WED. (The fact that this matches the engine numbers is just a happy co-incidence.) Having settled on the basic design, I designed some graphics that we could show for approval.

It's a rare occurrence that a group outside of the Company develops a "plus" for an attraction. As such, we needed to obtain permission from a number of entities, including Disneyland Park management and Walt Disney Imagineering. We were met with enthusiasm and support at each step through the approval process. Additionally, we solicited input and commentary from the group of people who best know and care for those engines: the crew of the Disneyland Railroad. Each group offered their suggestions on the style and content of the plate designs, and we are grateful for their support.

Although Walt Disney's family no longer owned the Disneyland Railroad — Retlaw Enterprises sold it and the Disneyland Monorail along with the rights to Walt Disney's name to the Walt Disney Company in 1982 — I still felt that it was appropriate to ask for his family's input on the project and for their permission to use the "Retlaw" name. I had successfully collaborated with Diane Disney Miller, Walt's daughter, and her family on various projects since the late 1990's, but I wasn't certain how they would react to this idea. Diane couldn't have been more enthusiastic about it! She liked the idea so much that she generously offered to pay for all of it. Disneyland had already allocated funds to this effort, so they didn't need additional support. However, I suggested an alternative way for Diane to show her support of the Railroad: we could create miniature pins of the builders plates and give these to current and past DLRR cast members.

Diane happily agreed to provide these and wrote a note of appreciation that was printed on a card to which the pins were affixed. She suggested that we make more sets that were necessary for the Disneyland Railroad so that they could be given to cast members at other Disney Parks as well. I had the unique privilege of personally presenting these pin sets to the engine crews at Disneyland, Walt Disney World, Tokyo Disneyland and Disneyland Paris. The crews were both surprised and deeply touched that Walt's family continues to appreciate the dedication of the cast members who keep, in Diane's words, "these giants running and looking gorgeous."

To fabricate the actual plates, we enlisted the help of Harry Van der Wyk of Hortie Van Innovations. Harry has a long history with Disneyland: he and his brother, Lyon, supplied all of the flagpoles, banner and bunting to the Park when it opened in 1955. In fact, Harry would occasionally have breakfast with Walt himself! The foundry that Harry used has been in business for over 100 years, and they crafted superb plates.

The plates were affixed to the C. K. Holliday and E. P. Ripley in November, 2005. Thanks to the immediacy of the Internet, Society members were able to see photos of the finished product shortly after they mounted.

This project was truly a team effort. In addition to the aforementioned individuals, I must recognize: Matt Ouimet, Todd Bruechert, Eric Kratzer, Jon Storbeck and Ellie Marlow of Disneyland; Marty Sklar, Joel Fritsche and Barbara Hastings of WDI; and Diane Miller, Walter Miller and Charles Wixom of the Walt Disney Family Foundation. A very special thanks goes to Ray Spencer, the Imagineer assigned to this project, as well as Dale Tetley and the rest of the DLRR roundhouse crew. This tribute could not have happened without the collected talent and effort of these people.

Now you know the back story of how we helped create a lasting tribute to the 50th "birthday" of the Disneyland Railroad. So, the next time you visit Disneyland, please keep an eye out for the builder's plates on the C. K. Holliday and E. P. Ripley. Out of the thousands of happy guests that day, you'll be one of a very select set who knows how they came to be.

DISNEY LEGEND
ROGER E. BROGGIE

Listed on the builder's plate of the E.P. Ripley is the name of Roger Broggie, the very first Disney Imagineer. I would like to thank Mr. Broggie's son, **Michael Broggie***, for providing me with a biography of his father from his outstanding book titled* Walt Disney's Railroad Story.

For almost a half-century, Disney's original Imagineer— Roger Broggie—worked in the entertainment industry. Among his many accomplishments were discovering the solutions for motion picture special effects, developing electronic robots that could sing and dance, and building transportation systems ranging from old-fashioned steam trains to futuristic monorails.

In 1939, Dick Jones was hired by Mickey Batchelder at Disney Studios. Jones insisted that he be allowed to hire Roger, who joined Walt Disney Productions as a precision machinist on October 1, 1939. The new Disney studio at Burbank was in its final phase of construction, and engineers were needed to move and adapt old animation cameras from the original location on Hyperion Avenue, in Los Angeles' Silverlake District, to the new facilities.

Roger's initial assignment was to install the complicated multi-plane animation equipment. Later he closely worked with Ub Iwerks, the Academy Award-winning designer of animation processes and camera equipment. Together, they developed rear-screen special effects, camera cranes, and high-speed optical printers: If Ub could imagine it, Roger would figure out a way to build it.

In 1950, Roger was promoted to department manager of the studio's machine shop, which had a staff of 12 machinists. Two years later, preliminary design work was commenced on Disneyland. A new company was formed called Walt Disney, Inc., to oversee the task. To avoid stockholder objections, the company's name was changed to WED Enterprises. Roger was one of WED's early leaders, selected by Walt Disney to guide Disneyland's development.

On October 18, 1990, Roger was honored by the Disney organization at a Disney Legend Awards ceremony along with six of his colleagues who "helped create the happiest place on Earth," in the words of company Chairman Michael Eisner. In recognizing Roger, Roy E. Disney—company co-chairman and nephew of Walt Disney—said, *"Any mechanical things you had to do, what you said was, 'Call Roger, he'll know how to fix it.' Without him, Disneyland wouldn't have happened."*

"NOTE" THE ORCHESTRION

This next secret is revealed for only one quarter.

It's easy to dismiss the antique "props" on stage in Disneyland as simply decorations, old artifacts from another era that may have performed a function at one time, but are now sitting idle as part of the background scenery. However, this is not the Disney way. Thousands of guests walk past this next Disneyland secret every day unaware that it is an original and fully functional piece of musical entertainment from the days when Mickey Mouse was being introduced to the world as Steamboat Willie.

Located next to the exit to the boarding platform at the Disneyland Railroad Main Street Station is a mint-condition Nelson-Wiggen Orchestrion, an "orchestra in a cabinet" manufactured in the mid-1920s. A spectacle of entertainment during its day, the inside features an elaborate collection of instruments, including drums, a piano, tambourine, mandolin, wood block, cymbal, triangle, castanets and a xylophone. Drop in a quarter while waiting for your train and enjoy some musical entertainment from the early days of Mickey Mouse!

Impersonating
The Ernest S. Marsh

Photo courtesy of Steve DeGaetano

The following article was graciously contributed by **Steve DeGaetano**, Disneyland Railroad Historian and author of the new book *Welcome Aboard The Disneyland Railroad! - A Complete History in Words and Pictures - Collector's Edition.* Learn more about this and his other books at www.SteamPassages.com

Most folks know the names of the five steam locomotives that circle Disneyland. No. 1, the *C.K. Holliday*; No. 2, the *E.P. Ripley*; No. 3, the *Fred Gurley*; No. 4, the *Ernest S. Marsh*, and No. 5, the *Ward Kimball*. But most people probably don't know that Engine No. 3 has worn *two different names* in its Disneyland career.

In June 1959, Disneyland was gearing up for what was then considered its second grand opening. The Matterhorn, the Disney-Alweg Monorail, and the Submarine Voyage were among several new adventures that could be enjoyed by the whole family. The Park's attendance had even skyrocketed enough to warrant the refurbishment of a fourth steam locomotive for the Santa Fe & Disneyland Railroad! The engine would be named after the Chairman of the Board of the real Santa Fe, Ernest S. Marsh.

To publicize the exciting summer of 1959, Disney prepared a 12 page all-color supplement that would appear in the local Sunday newspapers in early June. The supplement included concept drawings of the coming attractions, along with color photos of existing ones. Walt, of course, wanted to include a photo of his newest locomotive. Unfortunately, at press time, the *Ernest S. Marsh* was still very much in the process of being rebuilt—it wouldn't actually enter service at the Park until July 25.

But that didn't stop Walt! Understanding that perhaps most folks wouldn't know the difference, Disney had his artisans create a wooden name panel, with routed edges and notched corners, and the name *Ernest S. Marsh* proudly painted in red on the yellow background. For the photo session, this plaque was affixed to the cab side of Engine No. 3, obscuring the existing *Fred Gurley* name! As you can see in the photo, the engine number is still visible on the tender flank to the right. The caption touting the new "Ernest S. Marsh" highlighted the real Santa Fe's "crack" schedule of 39.5 hours between Los Angeles and Chicago.

So, for a few hours in 1959, the *Fred Gurley* impersonated the *Ernest S. Marsh*—the only Disneyland engine to have had two names while in service at Disneyland.

A HAUNTED DISNEYLAND ENGINE?

The following article was contributed by **Steve DeGaetano** from his new book *Welcome Aboard The Disneyland Railroad – A Complete History in Words and Pictures – Collector's Edition.* Learn more at www.SteamPassages.com

In addition to being the oldest, the *Fred Gurley* may also be the most haunted locomotive on the Disneyland line. It has been reported by several of the engine crews that on certain nights, when the weather is warm and the wind is calm, an unseen engineer rides along in the cab. As the *Gurley* pulls out of Toontown Station on evenings like this and rolls slowly past "it's a small world", the locomotive's bell has been known to start rocking gently back and forth, beginning slowly, but eventually ringing audibly - on its own, without ever having been touched by the hands of the "mortal" fireman or engineer! The track here is exceptionally smooth, and the *Gurley* is the only locomotive that behaves in this manner.

Al DiPaolo, an eight-year veteran Disneyland Railroad engineer and now a restorer at the California State Railroad Museum, states that it is possible to make the engine's bell ring due to the engine's short main rod, which, at certain speeds and cut-offs, can cause the locomotive to waddle or "hunt". Al has made the bell ring on many occasions in this manner. Another engineer, currently employed at the park, notes, however, that he has had the bell ring on its own while stopped at the station!

The following explanation is accepted by many of the Disney engine crews:

The *Fred Gurley* was the favorite locomotive of Harley Ward Ilgen. Harley and the *Gurley* were the same age, both having come into the world in 1894, so Harley's affection for the little engine is understandable. Harley was a personal friend of Walt's and first chief engineer of the Santa Fe & Disneyland Railroad in the 1950s. Incidents of the *Gurley's* bell ringing on its own began to occur shortly after Harley's death in August, 1963, and it is believed that the dearly departed chief engineer is merely tagging along for a ride in his favorite engine, announcing his presence by ringing the bell! Surely stranger things have happened in annals of railroad lore.

A MODEL OF WALT'S "LILLY BELLE"

As you enter the Disneyland Railroad Main Street Station, you'll see directly in front of you what many guests simply assume to be a model train used as a decoration, but it is far, far more than that. In fact, it's a tribute to Walt Disney's love of trains and a very important piece of Disneyland's history.

Of all the "rolling stock" Walt Disney ran on his "Carolwood Pacific" railroad in the backyard of his Holmby Hills home, none was more important to him than the "Lilly Belle" steam engine. Hand-built by Walt and Disney Imagineers, and named after his wife, Lillian, this detailed 1/8 scale reproduction of the Central Pacific #173 pulled guests riding atop trailing railcars along 2,615' of track, which wound its way around bends, over long trestles and even through a 90' tunnel under Lillian Disney's treasured flower beds.

The original Lilly Belle steam engine on display at the Walt Disney Family Museum in San Francisco

Stop inside the Disneyland Railroad Station in Town Square to see a full-sized model of Walt Disney's prized "Lilly Belle" steam engine and Tender, the very inspiration for the trains which today encircle Disney theme parks around the world.

BUILT IN ONLY ONE YEAR

As you step back into the Town Square, pause and take in everything around you. From the Disneyland Railroad Station and Main Street, U.S.A. to Sleeping Beauty Castle and all the magic beyond, all of it was built in just under one year, with most of the major construction occurring only seven months prior to Disneyland's opening day.

Walt Disney purchased all of the land, which consisted of orange groves and walnut orchards, from 17 different families by early 1954, and on July 21, 1954, construction of

Disneyland began with the removal of the very first trees from the property. Work continued at a fast pace until all of the buildings and attractions were constructed in time for Disneyland's grand opening on July 17, 1955.

"DISNEYLAND WILL NEVER BE COMPLETED" - *Walt Disney*

Disneyland has certainly changed over the years, but it isn't difficult to find many things which date back to its opening day of July 17, 1955. The real trick is to discover something which predates the park, something that was around before even the first plans were drawn and the first shovelful of dirt turned.

Admittedly, this next secret may not have a lot of "wow" to it, but it is definitely unique and will appeal to Disneyland fans. In mid-July of 1954, the McNeil Construction Company began their work at the new Disneyland construction site. Their first order of business was to clear the land, and this required the removal of 12,500 orange trees, 700 eucalyptus trees and 500 walnut trees. However, on your left as you enter the park, behind City Hall, you'll notice a stand of tall eucalyptus trees, which was never removed. It was originally planted as a windbreak for the orange groves and walnut orchards on the property, and Walt decided to keep it to create a visual barrier between Main Street, U.S.A. and The Jungle Cruise of Adventureland.

It's Your Birthday

Birthdays shouldn't be a secret at Disneyland, so start your day by stopping by City Hall and asking for your special birthday button. You'll enjoy well-wishes from cast members throughout your visit. Buttons are also available at other locations within the park, as well as the Reception desk of your Disneyland Resort hotel.

More Thought for Seed

If you're making your way through Disneyland and you spot a plant you just have to have in your own yard, stop by City Hall and ask to see the notebook which lists all of the plants used throughout Disneyland. Turning to the section for Fantasyland, you'll read...

"Upon walking through Sleeping Beauty Castle from the hub into the Castle Courtyard, it becomes immediately apparent that you've entered Fantasyland. This is a combination of children's fairy tales. The landscape reflects these make believe story lines; some are based on authentic locations and others on imagined lands. This is the only land that has topiary animals. Permanent shrub and perennial plantings range from formal to whimsical. The blooming color is bold."

ONLY FIVE MONTHS TO BUILD

Now take a moment to stand in the center of the Town Square and try to grasp the significance of this next secret. While all of Disneyland took just under one year to build, everything you see around you in the Town Square took only five months for its original construction. The Disneyland Railroad Station, City Hall, the entrance underpasses, landscaping, Fire Station, Disneyland Emporium, Main Street, U.S.A...all of it in only five months and in time for opening day.

"TO ALL WHO COME TO THIS HAPPY PLACE; WELCOME"

While in the center of the Town Square, stand over by the Flag Pole and notice the shiny bronze plaque at its base. It's a copy of the speech Walt delivered on the opening day of Disneyland...

"To all who come to this happy place; welcome. Disneyland is your land. Here age relives fond memories of the past...and here youth may savor the challenge and promise of the future. Disneyland is dedicated to the ideals, the dreams and the hard facts that have created America...with the hope that it will be a source of joy and inspiration to all the world."

DISNEYLAND'S FORCED PERSPECTIVE

Next, look closely at the architecture and facades of the nearby buildings for a secret trick of the eye. Disney Imagineers designed and built the facades of the buildings on the Town Square and Main Street, U.S.A., as well as Sleeping Beauty Castle, with an optical illusion called "Forced Perspective." By using this technique, they made the buildings appear to be taller than they actually are. The street level floors were built to full scale at 12 feet in height, while the second story was built slightly smaller at 10 feet and the third story smaller still at 8 feet. In addition, the windows of the second and third stories were built both narrower and shorter to further the illusion of height. On Sleeping Beauty Castle, guests will notice the "stones" at the base are much larger than those higher on the castle, and a study of the nearby Matterhorn reveals this same trick of the eye.

HONORING VETERANS

If you're a Veteran, stop by City Hall and inquire about participating in the daily Flag Retreat Ceremony in Town Square. Each evening, Disney officials escort a single guest to the flagpole in the center of the square for an honorary lowering of the flag. The ceremony lasts about 15 minutes and is a patriotic event the entire family will enjoy. The ceremony typically begins between 4:30 p.m. and 5:30 p.m., depending upon the time of year.

CITY HALL PERSPECTIVE

Now study the façade of City Hall. Do you notice anything different about it? Does its scale look different than any of the surrounding buildings?

All of the buildings of Town Square and Main Street, U.S.A. were built using "forced perspective," but City Hall was built with a more accurate scale so it could house the offices Walt and his team needed to manage the construction, operations and opening of Disneyland. After the park opened to tremendous success, these offices were used to manage the publicity and promotion of the new park.

TOWN SQUARE CANNONS

Walt spent much of his youth in the Midwest, where nearly every small town has a park, and in that park is usually a cannon dedicated to the town's war veterans. Of course, Main Street, U.S.A. is modeled after Walt's boyhood town of Marceline, Missouri, so it's only fitting that two cannons are located near the flag pole in the Town Square to honor the veterans who visit Disneyland.

Note: The two cannons on display are 3" Hotchkiss Mountain Guns, likely manufactured during the late 1800s in France. Weighing 570 lbs. each, their forged steel barrels could fire a projectile 2¼ miles.

WHERE IT ALL STARTED

This next secret is one which goes unnoticed by thousands of guests everyday, but one you surely will not want to miss.

Walt Disney used to take his daughters, Sharon and Diane, to Griffith Park in Los Angeles, where the girls loved to ride a carousel with colorful wooden horses. It was here that Walt sat by himself on a park bench on numerous occasions while watching his daughters and wondered why parents couldn't join their children in all the fun. According to Walt...

"It came about when my daughters were very young and Saturday was Daddy's day, so we'd start out and try to go someplace. I'd take them to the merry-go-round and I took them different places and as I'd sit while they rode the merry-go-round - sit on a bench, you know, eating peanuts - I felt that there should be something built, some kind of amusement enterprise, where the parents and the children could have fun together. So that's how Disneyland started."

Now stroll towards the entryway of "Great Moments with Mr. Lincoln" and step inside to find a park bench displayed in the foyer. This is the actual park bench Walt Disney sat upon when he first dreamed of the idea of

Disneyland, and nearby is one of the colorful horses from the actual merry-go-round his daughters used to ride.

All that is Disneyland, Disney's California Adventure, Walt Disney World Resort, Disney Cruise Line and Disney theme parks around the world came from an inspiring moment of thought on this very park bench. Or in other words... "It all started with a merry-go-round."

DON'T PASS THIS BY

As guests enter Disneyland, they're excited about a day of fantasy and adventure as they rush through Town Square and down Main Street, U.S.A. towards their favorite attraction. At the end of their day, they're often worn out from all of the fun they've had and are focused on leaving. As a result, thousands and thousands of guests walk right past this next Disneyland secret every day unaware it even exists.

When entering Disneyland, take a moment to enter the "Great Moments with Mr. Lincoln" attraction in the Town

Square and discover a wealth of original historical models and works of art used in the design and construction of Disneyland, including beautiful large-scale models of all of Disneyland Park, Sleeping Beauty Castle and Splash Mountain, as well as original Disneyland ticket books, artifacts, artwork and more.

THE CAPITOL OF DISNEYLAND

Nearby, in the center of the room, guests will notice a large and magnificently detailed model of our National Capitol Building. Many guests incorrectly assume this was designed and built by Disney Imagineers for the "Great Moments with Mr. Lincoln" attraction, but it actually has a history which pre-dates Disneyland by more than 20 years. What follows here is *the first-ever published account* of how this model was created, as well as how Walt came to own it.

Made of Caenstone, this highly detailed model was sculpted by Mr. George H. Lloyd. Born in March, 1879 in Llanelly, South Wales, Mr. Lloyd learned the skills of stone sculpting and engraving as a young man from his father before immigrating to Canada via steamship in 1907, eventually settling in Ottawa. Highly skilled at the art, he practiced his trade on such stately buildings as the Cathedral of St. John the Devine and The Rockefeller Church, both in New York, McGill University in Montreal, and the Canadian Parliament Building in Ottawa, Canada. Mr. Lloyd stated the inspiration for creating his model of the U.S. Capitol Building *"...came to me in 1918 when I saw a picture of the capitol in a Philadelphia paper. I didn't have time to work on the model until the depression when I was out of work."*

In 1932, only a few years after Mickey Mouse made his debut in Steamboat Willie and 23 years before Disneyland opened, 53 year-old Mr. Lloyd journeyed to Washington D.C. to meet with the Capitol's architect, Mr. David Lynn, where he explained his intent to

Cathedral of St. John the Devine - New York

carve an intricate miniature reproduction of the building out of Caenstone, a fine-grained limestone quarried from the Caen area of Normandy, France. Impressed by Mr. Lloyd's plans, Mr. Lynn graciously supplied him with pictures, drawings and blueprints, which would not only make the model easier to sculpt, but would ensure its accuracy, as well. With these materials in hand, Mr. Lloyd began the slow and deliberate task of hand-carving over 500 pieces out of stone, a process of intricate craftsmanship which would require many 16 hour days over the course of over three and a half years to finish, resulting in the magnificent structure we see today.

Photo courtesy of Jordan Sallis
Mr. Lloyd's great, great, great niece

In 1940, nearly five years after he had finished, Mr. Lloyd began to tour the country while displaying his Capitol model in the department stores of cities large and small, including Chicago, Memphis, Portland, Salt Lake City, San Francisco and Los Angeles, among others. In this era, during the remainder of the Great Depression and before the advent of widespread television, a patriotic and notable achievement such as this would be a form of quality entertainment, and people would journey from miles around to come see it. Eventually, millions of Americans did come to view its stately beauty, and one of those was Walt Disney himself. Being both patriotic and a fan of detailed miniatures, Walt engaged in correspondence with Mr. Lloyd about buying his model with the intention of putting it on display near the entrance of a new land he was adding to Disneyland, called "Liberty Street".

On October 18, 1955, Mr. Lloyd was displaying his model in Robinson's Department Store in Southern Los Angeles and wrote to Walt to see if "...*you are still interested in my replica of the National Capital*".(sic) Walt and Mr. Lloyd agreed to terms, and the following Monday, October 24, 1955, Walt had the U.S. Capitol Building model he wanted for "Liberty Street" in the Studio.

Mr. Lloyd would later write to his family...

Photo courtesy of Jordan Sallis

"*I displayed my work in Los Angeles...and sold it to a well known motion picture man named Walt Disney and it will be on permanent display at his wonderful exhibition grounds at Los Angeles.*"

Unfortunately, Liberty Street was never completed, yet the U.S. Capitol Building model was eventually displayed with the "Great Moments with Mr. Lincoln" attraction beginning in 1965, where it resides today, and its stately beauty has been enjoyed by millions of guests from around the world ever since.

Mr. Lloyd passed away in Palo Alto, California in May, 1962 at the age of 82.

Extremely rare June, 1944 brochure distributed by
Lowenstein's Department Store in Memphis, TN.
Author's Personal Collection

Mr. Lloyd's words from his WWII era promotional brochure titled, "George H. Lloyd's Hand Carved Caenstone Model of Our National Capitol"...

"I made up my mind to some day carve a model from stone and accordingly went to Washington D. C. where I met Mr. David Lynn, the Capitol architect, who treated me with great kindness. I explained my project and to my great delight, Mr. Lynn made available to me numerous photographs, drawings and blueprints that made the task much easier and insured accuracy. It has taken me 3 1/2 years to complete my model but I have enjoyed every minute of it, and feel that many thousands of people who have perhaps never visited the Capitol will look with interest and pleasure at this work."

Note: In writing this book, I wondered about the history of the miniature hand carved stone model of the U.S. Capitol Building on display within the Great Moments with Mr. Lincoln attraction, as well as the man who created it. Little to nothing about either was available anywhere, and the plaque affixed to the model at Disneyland offers only a small amount of information. I turned to the web to begin my research and there I found an image of an original World War II era brochure, which was for sale on eBay. Issued by Lowenstein's Department Store in Memphis, Tennessee, it promoted the display of the U.S. Capitol model by Mr. Lloyd in their store in June of 1944. That in itself was interesting, but even more so was the first-ever photo I had seen of Mr. Lloyd. Not only of Mr. Lloyd, but of Mr. Lloyd standing next to the very U.S. Capitol Building model now at Disneyland. This was truly a rare document tied to the history of Disneyland! I placed my bid and then began the wait for the auction to end. Would other people know the significance of this item? Would most people assume it's just an old brochure and overlook it? Does anyone even know who George H. Lloyd is? Thankfully, the auction ended and I was the sole bidder. The price I paid...$5.50.

As I had hoped, upon its receipt the brochure offered up a great deal of all new information about Mr. Lloyd, as well as additional clues to follow as part of my research. I am happy to share this with you in what is the *first-ever publication of this information and photos of Mr. Lloyd in any Disney-related content.*

Lastly, inside the brochure is a hand stamped address for Mr. Lloyd which reads...

GEORGE LLOYD
30 Irving Street
SAN FRANCISCO 22, CALIF.

In doing some follow up research with the Disney Archives, I learned they also have a copy of this brochure, but it does not have Mr. Lloyd's address stamp inside. This leads me to believe the brochure pictured above *may* have been owned at one time by Mr. Lloyd.

Note: I would like to recognize the contribution of Ms. Jordan Sallis, who, along with her grandfather, Brian Hillman, generously shared information and photos which greatly contributed to this story about the Capitol of Disneyland.

A LETTER OF NOTE

The mailboxes found throughout Disneyland? They're not just decorations, but instead are actual mailboxes. Drop in your letter and it'll soon arrive at its destination by U.S. Mail.

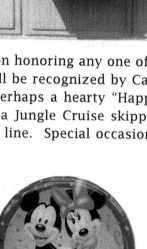

BE A V.I.P. AT DISNEYLAND

Want to be treated like a V.I.P. during your visit to Disneyland? Stop in at City Hall and pick up a button honoring any one of a number of special occasions, and you'll be recognized by Cast Members throughout your visit with perhaps a hearty "Happy Birthday!", a special recognition from a Jungle Cruise skipper or maybe an escort to the front of the line. Special occasions include...

* First Visit
* Happy Birthday
* I'm Celebrating
* Happy Anniversary
* Happily Ever After
* Just Graduated
* Just Engaged
* Just Married

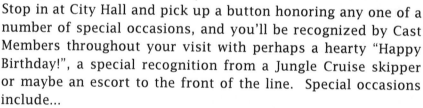

No Gum Allowed

Drum courtesy of Nelscott Antiques, Lincoln City, OR

One of the things guests appreciate about Disneyland is its cleanliness. It's a subtle thing, but a very important part of the story. Pay attention and you'll notice there isn't any gum spotting the sidewalks, stuck to the railings, found under chairs or sticking to the Cast Members' shoes as they perform in the parades. Why? Because gum isn't sold anywhere at Disneyland Resort.

Bank on Walt's Vault

Now make your way next door to the Disneyland Gallery. In addition to finding upscale works of Disney and Disneyland related art, you'll find a large bank vault dating back to 1904. Walt wanted a means by which guests could access cash to enjoy the activities of Disneyland, so Disneyland opened with the Bank of Main Street on this spot. Actually a Bank of America, its tellers provided all the services of a bank but with a Disneyland flair. With the advent of ATMs, however, the bank was closed in 1993 and it now houses the Disneyland Gallery. The secret? Find the massive bank vault door and peek inside the vault. There you will find the latest in an ever-changing display of rare and unique items relating to Disneyland, Walt Disney and The Walt Disney Company.

You'll find a nod to the original Bank of Main Street in a mural on the outside of the building, facing towards the Disneyland Railroad Main Street Station.

RED PAVERS

The red of the sidewalk pavers in Town Square and Main Street, U.S.A.? It was chosen to enhance the green of the foliage, as the two colors are opposites on the color wheel.

WALT DISNEY'S WINDOW

Guests visiting the Magic Kingdom at Walt Disney World in Florida often make a point of searching for the two windows honoring Walt Disney. One is the very first window guests see when entering the park, high atop the Magic Kingdom Railroad Station, and the other appears as the very last window on Main Street, U.S.A., facing towards Cinderella Castle.

Logically, one would assume Walt Disney would be honored in a similar fashion at Disneyland, but this isn't the case. There is no window to be found for Walt Disney on the Disneyland Railroad Station, Town Square or even Main Street, U.S.A. Instead, Walt Disney is honored with two windows atop the Library in Toontown, where Mickey Mouse lives. Note, however, that Walt is acknowledged with the lit lamp in his apartment above the Fire Station.

WALT IS IN THE PARK

This next secret is a warm and touching tribute to Walt Disney. During the building of Disneyland, Walt was frequently in the park overseeing every aspect of its construction, and this would require long hours morning to night,

day after day. To allow for more time on site, Walt had an apartment built on the second floor of the Disneyland Fire Station, and he and his family would stay there while Disneyland was being constructed. Decorated in a Victorian style featuring a red and green motif with rose accents, which were a favorite of Walt's wife, Lillian, the apartment was relatively small, with a main living room, sleeper sofas and a small kitchenette.

In time, everyone working on the construction of Disneyland came to realize that if the lamp in the window of Walt's apartment was lit, it meant Walt was in the park. To this day, the lamp always remains lit as an homage to Walt Disney and to give a sense that he is somewhere in Disneyland, directing another part of its unfinished story.

A PRIVATE VIEW OF DISNEYLAND

If you look up and to the left of Walt's Apartment, when facing it from Town Square, you'll notice a lattice-faced deck behind a large Chinese Banyan tree. This was Walt and Lillian's private deck off their apartment, which they used for family events, to host guests and to watch the magic of Disneyland when they had a rare quiet moment.

SAY "CHEESE"

Walt Disney grew up when times were tough, and his early years in business were quite lean. As a result, he learned to enjoy the simple things in life, and when it came to food, he had three favorites...a good bowl of chili with beans, toasted cheese sandwiches and, of course, ice cream.

In a touch of Disney whimsy, a "tribute" to these three items can be found on Main Street, U.S.A. today, just as they were in 1955. Step inside the Carnation Cafe and you'll find "Walt's Chili" on the menu for lunch or dinner. Now make your way to the Jolly Holiday Bakery and you'll find toasted cheese sandwiches hot off the grill, and once you've finished, stop in at the Gibson Girl Ice Cream Parlor to enjoy Walt's favorite dessert in the form of a cone, shake or sundae.

Note: If you're lucky enough to visit Walt's apartment above the Disneyland Fire Station as part of a tour, you'll see in the kitchenette the small 1934 General Electric grill Walt used to make his own toasted cheese sandwiches.

INTERNATIONAL STREET

Photo courtesy of www.davelandweb.com

"Disneyland will never be completed. It will continue to grow as long as there is imagination left in the world."
                                        - Walt Disney

Walt knew his new Disneyland had to continually grow and change so as to always provide magical new experiences for his guests with each and every visit. Seventeen different attractions welcomed guests on opening day in 1955, but of course many more would follow as Disneyland's story continued to unfold, including Dumbo the Flying Elephant, the Matterhorn Bobsleds, "it's a small world", Pirates of the Caribbean, the Haunted Mansion and many others. Unfortunately, two of Walt's ideas never came to fruition; International Street and Liberty Street.

Before you head down Main Street, U.S.A. towards Sleeping Beauty Castle, make your way towards the Mad Hatter and take note of the short "road spur" in front of the shop. Today, this road leads to a backstage area, but in 1955 Walt had plans for it to lead to an all new "land" in the park, one called International Street.

Like Main Street, U.S.A., but with an international flavor instead of old-fashioned American, International Street would allow guests to walk its narrow winding street amidst shops, restaurants and exhibits from around the world, as well as enjoy entertainment with an international flair. Many feel International Street was a precursor of Epcot's World Showcase, as guests would've moved "from country to country" as they made their way along. However, just as International Street began to materialize in its planning and construction phase, Walt would begin production on a new Disney movie about the revolutionary times in Colonial America, titled "Johnny Tremain", which caused him to think of a different use for this space...a new land he would call "Liberty Street."

LIBERTY STREET

Photo courtesy of www.davelandweb.com

Walt was very appreciative and respectful of our country's heritage, and he sought to reflect this in his new Disneyland. On opening day in July, 1955, he had included both Town Square and Main Street, U.S.A., two attractions which reflect a time in America's history of simple, honest values, as well as Frontierland, with its nod to the courage of discovery in the old West.

In September of 1956, a little over a year after Disneyland had opened, Walt began production on a new movie titled "Johnny Tremain", which told the story of a young man by the same name who worked as a silversmith apprentice in Boston alongside Paul Revere. Set in Colonial America in the year 1775, Johnny plays an important role in a number of famous events which culminated in the American Revolution, including the Boston Tea Party and Paul Revere's ride warning "The British are coming!"

In reading the story as preparation for the film, Walt realized he had made an oversight in planning his new theme park...

"After reading Johnny Tremain, we realized we had overlooked one major item in the blueprint of Disneyland. A memorial to the freedoms that made it all possible."

With this, Walt began to rethink his plans for what was then International Street off of Town Square. He realized he now wanted this street to be a representation of Colonial America, an area of the park in which guests could acquire an understanding and appreciation of the Revolutionary War, our nation's Presidents, how enterprise helped shape our great country and the dramatic struggles and events which won us all liberty and freedom. Walt said...

"Liberty Street will be Johnny Tremain's Boston of about 1775."

Designed as a cul-de-sac instead of a long winding street, Liberty Street would welcome guests with a collection of attractions, shops and exhibits which immersed them in colonial times. A glass shoppe would feature working glass smiths hand blowing colorful pieces of art, while nearby a blacksmith would be practicing his trade, and of course, Paul Revere's Silver Shop would welcome guests with the finest examples in the art of Silversmithing.

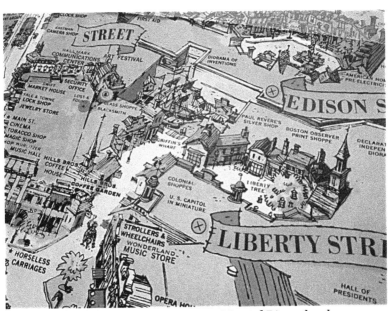

1962 Sam McKim Souvenir Map of Disneyland
Author's Personal Collection

Two authentic three-masted ships at Griffin's Wharf would "anchor" one end of Liberty Street, while stately Liberty Hall would majestically reside at the other. Inside, a show titled, "One Nation Under God", would feature Walt's earliest attempts at Audio-Animatronic figures of our nation's Presidents, a technology which he would soon perfect and reveal to the world at The Enchanted Tiki Room in 1963 and the 1964 New York World's Fair.

While Liberty Street was never built, many of Walt's concepts and dreams for this land were developed for use elsewhere in Disneyland and all throughout Liberty Square in Walt Disney World's Magic Kingdom.

CHAPTER TWO

SECRETS OF
MAIN STREET, U.S.A.

"For those of us who remember the carefree time it recreates, Main Street will bring back happy memories. For young visitors, it is an adventure in turning back the calendar days of their grandfather's youth."

- Walt Disney

A Moment in History

Before you begin your stroll down Main Street, U.S.A., take a moment to realize the era in which you're standing. While many guests assume they're simply surrounded by an old-fashioned turn of the 20th century  town, they're actually immersed in a moment in history which represents the dawn of the Industrial Revolution and the advent of electricity. Gas lamps are being replaced with electric bulbs, horse-drawn trolleys share the road with new motorized jitneys, the loud whistles of powerful steam trains fill the air and the street itself is busy with the hustle and bustle found in old photos of this era.

The Arrival of Electricity

As you make your way down Main Street, U.S.A., you are actually "traveling through time", in a sense, and one of the visual clues the Disney Imagineers use to convey this illuminating story element are the historic street lamps.

Main Street, U.S.A. represents turn-of-the-20th century America, and more specifically Marceline, Missouri, Walt's boyhood hometown. As such, it is lined with old-fashioned street lamps, all of which have a single gas flame. In the days of old, all street lamps were powered by gas, and each evening men known as

"Lamplighters" would make their way from lamp to lamp to light the lamps as darkness approached. Since Main Street, U.S.A. captures a time of transition in America's history, notice how the street lamps change as you leave Main Street, U.S.A. and make your way into the Hub in front of Sleeping Beauty Castle. Here, instead of a single elegant flame, each lamppost now uses the latest technology...an incandescent light bulb powered by the "new" electricity of the era.

An Old-Fashioned Deal

The Disneyland gas street lamps? They're authentic and well over 150 years old. With gas lamps having been replaced with electric lamps featuring new incandescent bulbs, the City of Baltimore, Maryland was selling the lamps as scrap for $.03 cents per pound back in 1955, the same year Disneyland opened. Disneyland and Walt Disney World designer Emile Kuri purchased the lamps and gave them a new home on Main Street, U.S.A.

The Gibson Girl Ice Cream Parlor

Throughout Disneyland you'll find tributes to individuals who greatly influenced Walt Disney's life...the colorful antique Mutoscopes acknowledge animator Winsor McCay, a window on Main Street, U.S.A. recognizes Walt's father, Elias Disney, and with every frozen scoop of one of Walt's favorite treats, The Gibson Girl Ice Cream Parlor pays tribute to Charles Gibson.

Charles Dana Gibson was a skilled American illustrator best known for creating the "Gibson Girl", his personification of a woman who embodied feminine beauty and confidence during the late 19th and early 20th centuries, the period of Main Street, U.S.A. His exceptional skills as an illustrator, especially those that conveyed the expressions of the human face in his prodigious work, were recognized and appreciated by millions around the world, including a young Walt Disney.

In addition, during WWI, Mr. Gibson led the Division of Pictorial Publicity for the Committee on Public Information, an agency of the government charged with influencing the public's opinion about the war. In this role, Mr. Gibson was involved with assisting military recruitment, and as such he lent his notable creation, the Gibson Girl, to those efforts, including in a poster which encouraged young men to serve in WWI as ambulance drivers in France. Coincidentally, this was the position Walt held after joining the Red Cross Ambulance Corp at the age of 16, in which he spent one year in France, from 1918 to 1919, driving supplies from warehouses to hospitals and canteens in and around Paris, as well as the surrounding French countryside.

Of note is that only two Disney theme parks in the world include a Gibson Girl Ice Cream Parlor; Disneyland and, of course, Disneyland Paris.

THE OMNIBUS
THREE SECRETS IN ONE!

It's easy to overlook the Omnibus as a less-than-thrilling experience, especially when compared to the Pirates of the Caribbean, Splash Mountain or Space Mountain, but hop aboard this classic attraction, which dates back to the early days of Disneyland, and it may quickly become one of your new favorites...or perhaps three!

1) As you enter Disneyland, find the Omnibus in the Town Square, climb to the upper deck via the back stairs and sit in the front seat, which faces forward over the cab. Once the Omnibus departs and begins to slowly make its way towards Sleeping Beauty Castle, you'll have an exciting V.I.P. view of Main Street, U.S.A. from high in the air as it all unfolds in front of you. In fact, it's almost as if you're the star of your very own Disneyland parade float!

2) From your new high perspective, you'll have more of an eye-level view of the tributes adorning the windows of Main Street, U.S.A., which not only makes them easier to read, but it's great for photographing them, too.

3) Have you ever stood near the "Partners" statue of Walt and Mickey and wished you could get an unobstructed photo of Sleeping Beauty Castle, one without people in the foreground? With a front row seat on the upper deck of the Omnibus, now you can. Have your camera ready as the Omnibus makes its way down Main Street, U.S.A. and approaches the Hub. Just before it begins a slight turn to the right, *you'll realize you're now about 12' high, right in the middle of Main Street, U.S.A.* and well above all the guests' heads. Perfect for getting a classic photo of Sleeping Beauty Castle. Be ready, as the opportunity lasts only a moment, and if you miss it...well then, it's just an excuse to ride again!

WALT'S BRIGHT IDEA

One of the elements which makes Main Street, U.S.A. magical is the lighting on the buildings. Here's a story from Bob Gurr about how the idea for rim lights came about from Walt Disney...

"In 1955, when the Christmas season came around, Walt asked the guys down at the park to put some lighting up on top of the buildings, because there's a lot of architectural detail, and we referred to that as 'rim lighting', like across the top of a rim of a roof or something. We put up white lights, and then Walt said, 'Gee, that looked kind of nice. Let's turn that into colored lights for Christmas.' So that was the first inkling of "Yes, you could do more than just have buildings. You could actually light them up, and of course, as you know, ever since we've had rim lighting on all the buildings."

My thanks to the folks at the Mousestalgia.com podcast for their permission to use this illuminating secret.

MAIN STREET, U.S.A.
WINDOW DISPLAYS

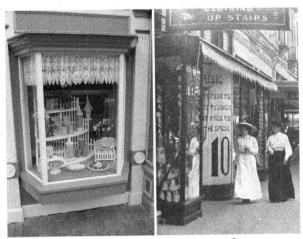

Historical photo courtesy of
Main Street, U.S.A. in Early Photographs
- Dover Publications, Inc.

You'll often hear that Walt designed the storefront windows of Main Street, U.S.A. to be low so that even small children could easily look inside and see their magical displays, but this is actually a "Disneyland urban legend." Instead, the low window displays are another example of the Imagineers' attention to detail.

Main Street, U.S.A. represents turn-of-the-20th-century America. In this era, before the Internet, television and even radio, shop owners had to rely upon their window displays as their primary means of advertising. As a result, they typically built them as large as they could, often reaching nearly to the sidewalk so as to show off as much merchandise as possible to passing customers.

DISNEY THEME PARKS BY MAIL

Did you know you can buy the very same merchandise found on Main Street, U.S.A. and throughout Disney Theme Parks at home?

Want to adorn the entire family in Disneyland t-shirts before flying to your favorite vacation destination? Feel like celebrating a birthday at home while wearing Mickey Mouse ears? Forget to buy that special souvenir before you left the parks?

Now you can! Disney offers a magical selection of merchandise from its different theme parks through a variety of shopping methods, including online at www.DisneyParks.com/store, its Shop Disney Parks mobile app, Merchandise Guest Services at 877-560-6477 and email: merchandise.guest.services@disneyparks.com

A FREE REPLACEMENT

Many guests already know that if they lose or pop a balloon while at Disneyland, they need only to ask a balloon vendor for a replacement, and they will receive a new one free of charge.

However, few guests know that if they break a souvenir, such as a sword or ceramic mug, they may also receive a free replacement, provided they still have their original receipt. In addition, guests who purchase a souvenir at one shop, but decide they'd much rather have a different souvenir while browsing at another shop, may show their receipt, pay any price difference and exchange the souvenir. To make things easier, the guest may leave their old souvenir at the location where they purchase their new item.

CIGAR STORE INDIAN

As you enter Main Street, U.S.A. from the Town Square, take note of the statue of a Native American in front of the 20th Century Music Company storefront. A turn-of-the-century form of marketing, a "Cigar Store Indian" such as this visually conveyed to the public the services of the store in front of which it was placed, much like the striped barber pole indicated a barber, or a large tooth, like that found on Disneyland's Center Street, indicated the services of a dentist.

Why is this Cigar Store Indian here? It's because the original occupant of the 20th Century Music Company store was a "Fine Tobacco" shop. Sandwiched between the Magic Shop and the Main Street Cinema, it offered Disneyland guests quality tobacco from around the world from opening day in July, 1955 until June 3rd, 1990. You'll find a similar Cigar Store Indian in Frontierland by the Shooting Exposition.

Note: According to the Disney Archives, the Cigar Store Indians do not have names.

Photo courtesy of Van Eaton Galleries

Note: The Cigar Store Indian you see here is nearly 6' tall and is the original Cigar Store Indian which appeared in front of the Frontierland Trading Post in the 1960s. According to the Van Eaton Galleries, which auctioned this Cigar Store Indian in March of 2015... *"Frontierland's first citizen, well-known landmark and popular photo subject was this Cigar Store Indian, who stood watch in front of the Frontierland Trading Post for years. There were always two Cigar Store Indians at Disneyland, a red-caped one in front of the Main Street Tobacco Store, and a green caped one in Frontierland. Originally sculpted at the Disney Studio, a mold for fiberglass castings ("pulls") was created so that the Indians could be replaced after wear and tear from use in the park. To this day, "pulls" are made from the original molds and are still in place at Disneyland."*

THE WINDOWS OF
MAIN STREET, U.S.A.

As you continue to make your way up Main Street, U.S.A., take notice of the windows on the building facades.

Disneyland Resort, as well as all that is The Walt Disney Company, is the result of the vision, genius and determination of one man, Walt Disney. However, no man can do it all by himself, and Walt Disney was assisted by many talented and hard working Walt Disney Imagineers, Cast Members and others through the years in not only bringing about his dream, but keeping it alive for generations to come. Planners, architects, artists, animators, actors, graphic designers, project managers, singers, songwriters, costumers, even pony ride managers have all played a role in bringing

about all that is Disneyland Resort and The Walt Disney Company.

Many of these Disney Imagineers, Cast Members and others are honored with a window on Main Street, U.S.A. or elsewhere in the park. Having a window in your name at Disneyland is considered one of the highest honors in the company.

Tip: Hop aboard the Omnibus and climb to the top deck for a much better view of the windows as you travel down Main Street, U.S.A.

Elias Disney's Window

As you continue your stroll up Main Street, U.S.A. towards Sleeping Beauty Castle, you'll notice a window on the left which reads Elias Disney – Contractor. This is a tribute to Walt Disney's father, Elias, who held a number of different jobs in his lifetime, including that of a contractor. In fact, Elias built a home designed by Walt's mother, Flora, on the corner of Tripp Avenue and Palmer Street in Chicago, IL, and it was here that both Walt and his brother Roy, were born.

Learn about the restoration of Walt's birthplace at www.WaltDisneyBirthplace.org.

MAIN STREET CINEMA

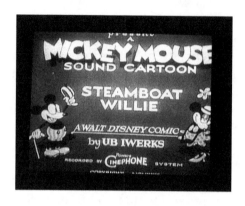

Now step past Tilly the Ticket Taker and catch this next secret playing at the Main Street Cinema.

If you were to ask someone the name of Mickey Mouse's first cartoon, chances are they will tell you it was *Steamboat Willie*. While this is a good answer, it's actually incorrect. On May 15, 1928, Walt Disney gave a test screening in Hollywood of Mickey Mouse's very first cartoon, *Plane Crazy*, a silent film inspired by the daring adventures of Charles Lindberg, who, in 1927, became the first man to make a non-stop solo flight across the Atlantic ocean. Unfortunately, as a silent film, and perhaps because nobody had ever heard of Mickey Mouse at that point, the film failed to pick up a distributor. Walt, realizing the importance of sound, introduced Mickey Mouse to the world six months later, on November 18, 1928, in the first synchronized post-produced sound cartoon, *Steamboat Willie*. These two cartoons not only introduced Mickey Mouse the world, but also launched Disney Cartoons and what would become The Walt Disney Company, the largest media and entertainment company in the world.

Note: According to the Disney Archives, Mickey Mouse's birth date "...*has always been determined to be the date that Steamboat Willie opened at the Colony Theater.*", which was November 18, 1928.

(By the way, did you happen to notice Tilly's hometown on her name badge? How about the illuminated Hidden Mickeys on the set of stairs inside?)

A PRICELESS CHEAP SILHOUETTE

Mistakenly overlooked by new guests, and plenty of old-timers, as well, the Silhouette Studio on Main Street, U.S.A. creates custom hand-cut portraits of guests, in silhouetted profile, which they can frame and enjoy as a personal and truly unique souvenir of their visit. Parents all across the world hold silhouettes created of their children on Main Street, U.S.A. as some of their most treasured possessions.

While highly valued by guests, the silhouette art form actually has a history of being considered "cheap". In March, 1759, Monsieur Etienne de Silhouette was named as Controller-General of France, where he enacted measures of austerity in order to gain control of the country's finances. Unfortunately, this gave him the reputation of being a penny-pincher. About that same time, a new and inexpensive art form was beginning to be displayed in homes by those who could not afford more expensive artwork, such as paintings or sculptures, and this new art form consisted of simply a dark image of an object displayed on a light background. Those who considered this to be an inexpensive form of art started referring to it as a "silhouette", indicating it was as cheap as Monsieur Etienne de Silhouette. Through time the name took hold, and this is why, more than 250 years later, we refer to this art form on Main Street, U.S.A. as a silhouette.

BORN AT DISNEYLAND

Next, step outside the Market House and look for the window honoring Ron Dominguez. It states...

"Orange Grove Property Mgt. - 'We'll Care For Your Property As If It Were Our Own' - Ron Dominguez, Owner."

The windows of Main Street, U.S.A. honor those individuals who made a significant contribution to the success of The Walt Disney Company or Disneyland Resort, as well as those who are notable to Walt, such as the window for Elias Disney, Walt Disney's father. In this case, the Orange Grove Property Mgt. window honors Ron Dominguez, and with its unique backstory, it stands out from the rest.

A little over one year before Disneyland opened in 1955, the land upon which Disneyland sits consisted of acres and acres of orange groves and walnut orchards. A total of 17 families owned all of the property, and Walt Disney bought it all for his new theme park idea. One of the property owners was Mr. and Mrs. Dominguez, who had a home situated about where the entrance to the Pirates of the Caribbean sits today, and they sold their 10-acre orange grove to Walt in 1954. Their 19 year-old son, Ron Dominguez, who had been born in their home on August 10th, 1935, went to work for Walt Disney as a ticket taker only four days before the park opened in 1955. In time, he rose through the ranks to become VP of Disneyland, before continuing on to accept the position of Executive Vice President, Walt Disney Attractions, West Coast.

It is because of this background that the window for the Orange Grove Property Mgt. promises to "care for your property as if it were our own."

SOUNDS LIKE
MORE DISNEYLAND FUN

This next secret is only for those who stop and listen. Pass by too quickly, and you're sure to miss it.

Duck down the side street at the Market House and head towards the end of the street for a fun audio secret. Sit down and wait for a while, and you'll hear the comical daily happenings of three different businesses.

At the small Hotel Marceline, you'll hear guests getting ready for the day, and in one instance Mr. Landers is scolded for using his noisy cylinder player in the house. Across the way, an unlucky patient is under the care of E.S. Bitz, D.D.S., the "Painless Dentist", though you wouldn't know it from the sounds of extreme discomfort coming from the dentist's office! And up above, piano lessons are being offered to a student who seems to get much better once the instructor leaves the room.

A Brick Wall
From Opening Day

Now look towards the end of the street and you'll find a brick wall with a drinking fountain in the middle of it. Notice anything odd about it? If you study it closely, you'll find three different types of bricks making up this one wall. Legend has it that this wall was built during Disneyland's construction so as to test different brick patterns for use within the park. Was it simply rushed to completion to close off the street with whatever bricks were left over in the final crazy days of Disneyland's construction? Were Imagineers really testing brick patterns, and if so, where were they used in the park? It's a mystery, but each year passes and the wall remains.

Original
Opening Day Orchestrion

One of the fun things about this Disneyland secret is discovering something which not only reaches back to opening day in 1955, but also ties directly to Walt Disney himself.

Walk over to the Penny Arcade and make your way to the back to discover the large Welte, Style 4 Orchestrion that's been at Disneyland since opening day in 1955. Manufactured in 1907 by M. Welte & Söhne in Freiburg, Germany, this elaborate antique provided the kind of musical entertainment enjoyed by Walt Disney as a child. Its collection of instruments performs once every seven minutes and showcases 265 pipes, as well as a bass drum, snare drum, timpani, triangle and cymbal, all while playing 75 key Welte roll music. Walt purchased this in 1953, and in 1955 it was installed in the Penny Arcade, where it's been entertaining guests ever since...just as Walt intended.

Note: It's an industry tradition for those who build or repair an instrument such as this to sign their names on an interior panel. For this particular instrument, the Disneyland Electromechanical team keeps this tradition alive by signing their names whenever major refurbishments are performed, which can be once a decade or longer.

An Old-Fashioned Party Line

Now step into the nearby Market House and look for five old-fashioned phones located on the walls throughout the establishment. More than just props, go ahead and pick up a receiver to eavesdrop on an entertaining conversation from the year 1890.

Note: The phone pictured here is a Western Electric Picture Frame Front Model 317 Cathedral Top Wall Telephone.

Antique Mutoscopes

Here's a secret which takes you back to another time for some old-fashioned fun, all for only a penny.

While in the Penny Arcade, you'll find three brightly painted antique cast iron "Clamshell" mutoscopes. Introduced in 1895, the mutoscope was one of the most popular machines in penny arcades across the country and provided customers with a form of moving entertainment before the era of motion pictures. Though they were wildly popular in their day, mutoscopes such as these are extremely rare now. If you were to find one, chances are it wouldn't work, so this is truly a once-in-a-lifetime opportunity to see this unique form of turn-of-the-20th century entertainment. Simply drop in a penny, peek into the viewer and turn the crank to watch an exciting, albeit brief, old movie.

Note: It's surprising to discover that the Mutoscope, while patented by Herman Casler in 1894, was invented by none other than Winsor McCay, who played an important role in the life of Walt

Disney. Inside each machine are over 800 cards, each of which is printed with a photographic image from approximately 50 feet of film, and these cards "flip" by rapidly as the user turns the crank. This is a process which is very similar to that of animated film, in which countless animated stills appear in rapid succession so as to give the illusion of fluid movement. It's only logical that Winsor McCay would go on to develop and publish in 1914 what is widely believed to be one of the very first animated films ever created, *Gertie the Dinosaur*. This is the film which is recognized by The Walt Disney Company as having played an important role in inspiring a young 12 year-old Walt Disney to become an animator.

WALT DISNEY'S BABY PHOTO

Since it's tucked inside the Disneyland Baby Center, this next secret is rarely seen, and even the few who do notice it may not realize whom it is they are seeing in the photo. Inside the front door of the Disneyland Baby Center, which is to the right at the end of Main Street, U.S.A., is a framed baby picture of Walt Disney at about 10 months of age.

THE LITTLE RED WAGON

As you step out of the Disneyland Baby Center, you'll notice a line of guests waiting at the Little Red Wagon parked on East Plaza Street. Serving some of the finest hand-dipped corn dogs you'll ever enjoy, the Little Red Wagon is more than just a "food cart", but instead a nod to the Red Wagon Inn, an upscale restaurant featuring full course meals and dating back to opening day in 1955. Known as Walt's favorite restaurant in the park, it occupied the space of the nearby Plaza Inn until 1965.

EDISON SQUARE

1962 Souvenir Map of Disneyland
Author's Personal Collection

As you stand on Plaza Street, you may be wondering, "Where does it go?" The answer?...To an important piece of Disneyland history that never was.

Walt Disney had imagined at the end of Plaza Street a walk-through attraction he called Edison Square, which was to be a tribute to Thomas A. Edison, the prolific American inventor who not only changed the face of the world and the course of history, but also invented many of the technologies which helped Walt bring his stories to life, including the motion picture camera, recorded music and the phonograph.

In a WED proposal to General Electric, Walt Disney explained his vision for Edison Square...

"*Edison Square in Disneyland will dramatically present the story of the way in which one invention by Thomas A. Edison has influenced the growth and development of America...Edison Square is the story of that era: the birth, growth, development and future of electricity and General Electric products.*

Located just a few steps from Main Street, Edison Square will be the passing of the 'old' of the 19th century to the 'new' of the 1900s. As they enter Progress Place in Edison Square, where they will find that 'Progress Is Our Most Important Product', visitors will see two separate plaques on which General Electric's symbol and appropriate words setting forth the theme of Edison Square will appear.

Inside the buildings, General Electric's theatrical productions will be staged for Disneyland visitors. Edison Square will be alive and vital. Disneyland's horseless carriages' and surreys which travel up and down Main Street will move in and out of the area. Such annual Disneyland special events as the 'Horseless Carriage Day Parade' and the 'Easter Parade' will be part of Edison Square.

The square itself will be architecturally landscaped befitting the turn-of-the-century. It will contain the 'new' electric lamps, iron grill work, hitching posts and other 'signs of the times.' All the windows in the buildings will be authentically dressed and specially lighted to carry out the atmosphere of the area."

Among the many wonders Walt wanted to showcase in Edison Square was a life-sized statue of Thomas Edison, something no doubt similar to the "Partners" statue of Walt and Mickey Mouse found today in front of Sleeping Beauty Castle.

An Illuminated Disneyland Secret

Tucked up and out of the way, this classic Disneyland secret is one which is missed by thousands and thousands of guests every day.

Visit the entrance to the Coca-Cola Refreshment Corner and take note of the alternating red and white light bulbs in the ceiling forming a closed loop. Since there is an odd number of sockets available, the Imagineers were faced with a bit of a conundrum...do they finish with two white bulbs side by side or two red bulbs? As you can see, the problem was solved when they decided to whimsically paint one bulb both red and white, thus preserving the sequence!

The History of the Partners Statue

The following is an excerpt from an article written by Disney historian Jim Korkis for MousePlanet.com. Jim has graciously shared it with us here...

Just two decades after his passing Walt Disney was being forgotten by a new generation of children who had grown up without seeing him on television every week.

Disney Legend Blaine Gibson, who knew and worked with Walt Disney closely during the last years of his life, was chosen to sculpt a permanent memorial to a man and his mouse to be placed at Disneyland.

"It started one day when Marty Sklar called me on the phone and asked if I'd be interested in doing a life-size statue of Walt, holding Mickey's hand," recalled Gibson in a 1995 interview. *"I chose to depict Walt as he was in 1954. I think that was when Walt was in his prime."*

Gibson made the figure of Walt larger than life, roughly 6-feet, 5-inches tall.

The size of Mickey Mouse was chosen based on a brief moment from the animated short *The Pointer* (1939). When Walt Disney was recording Mickey's voice as he faced a massive bear, he instinctively reached out to indicate that Mickey was roughly three feet tall in comparison to the ferocious bruin. From that moment on, that became Mickey's official height.

More than 7,000 economically challenged children from different countries were at Disneyland on November 18,1993 for a huge event called "Mickey's Worldwide Kids Party". These children were the guests of honor at the celebration of Mickey's 65th birthday and the official unveiling of the "Partners" statue.

Jack Lindquist, the President of Disneyland, officiated the ceremony. He spoke briefly and then introduced Roy E. Disney whose warm words charmed the audience.

Then in the front of the platform, the Fab Five (Mickey, Minnie, Donald, Goofy, Pluto) appeared and a huge curtain was dropped to reveal the statue.

There was a plaque by the statue that remains there today: *"I think most of all what I want Disneyland to be is a happy place...Where parents and children can have fun, together. —*

Walt Disney" At the Magic Kingdom at Walt Disney World the plaque states: *"We believe in our idea: a family park where parents and children could have fun — together. — Walt Disney."*

Disney sculptor Blaine Gibson told the media at the unveiling in 1993:

"Walt gave me and many others some of the happiest times of our lives, and this project was important because it wasn't just for Walt...it was about Walt."

"Our faces are all we really have that can tell people who we are. Many people asked me what Walt might be saying as he stood there with Mickey, and the expression I tried to capture was Walt saying to Mickey, 'Look what we've accomplished together', because truly they were very much a team through it all."

SMOKE TREE RANCH

Now study the tie Walt is wearing with the Partners statue. Look closely and you will see a symbol made up of three letters, "STR". These letters refer to the Smoke Tree Ranch in Palm Springs, California. Walt and his wife, Lillian, greatly enjoyed visiting the ranch whenever Walt could take a break from his many different projects. In fact, they enjoyed it so much that they chose to build a home there, but Walt sold it soon after its construction to help fund the building of Disneyland. It was a wise decision, as Disneyland proved to be such a success that he later built a new home at Smoke Tree Ranch, one which was even larger than the original.

A Unique Disneyland Moment

Stand to the side of Main Street, U.S.A. at the end of the day and you're sure to see the thousands and thousands of guests who clog the street as they exit the park, making sure they're out by the published closing time. This next secret gives you an opportunity for a unique Disneyland experience all these other guests miss.

Unbeknownst to these thousands of leaving guests, Disneyland is actually open for one hour each day *after the published park closing time* to allow guests to make their way towards Main Street, U.S.A. and do any last-minute souvenir shopping. For those who do not want to shop, they may leisurely make their way through their favorite land or perhaps occupy a quiet bench as they watch Disneyland slowly wind to a close after another day of magic and adventure.

A Last Minute Ride

Disneyland's extra hour after the published park closing time is an excellent opportunity to get in one or more rides on your favorite attraction. While other guests begin leaving the park early, make sure to head to your favorite attraction and *be in line by the published park closing time.*

Any guests in the queue at the time of the published park closing will be allowed to ride. Get there early enough, and you may be able to get in a few rides before the queue is closed, since so many other guests will have already left.

CHAPTER THREE

SECRETS OF ADVENTURELAND

"To create a land that would make this dream a reality, we pictured ourselves far from civilization, in the remote jungles of Asia and Africa."

- Walt Disney

FUR THE BIRDS, TUPPENCE A BAG

Photo courtesy of Dave Drumheller

Opening in June of 1963, Walt Disney's Enchanted Tiki Room was the first attraction to include Walt's new Audio-Animatronic technology, allowing a cast of over 150 talking, singing and dancing birds to entertain guests in a Polynesian setting.

Have you ever wondered how Disneyland's Figure Finishing Department adorned all the Audio-Animatronic birds in their bright plumage such that they could move and still appear as real birds? 30 year Imagineer Cindy Bothner explains the process in this interview, which is reprinted here with her kind permission...

"Fur and feathering a Tiki Bird is quite involved. If I remember correctly, it takes about 36 hours, maybe less after you get the hang of it. First, you are given a fiberglass and kydex (an alternate to leather) bird body. A pattern is made of muslin for the fur cloth, or bird fur. The pattern has to allow for the movement of the head, but still be snug enough so as not to bunch up and look fake. Very tricky!

You also have to craft a spandex collar that is glued to the neck opening, which keeps the bird fur from folding into the neck area when the bird moves. You then cut out the fur cloth according to the pattern. Before gluing it on, you paint the cloth the desired colors, which are air-brushed on with permanent ink. The face and feet are then painted with water-based acrylics. After the painting, you glue on the fur cloth and then feather the wings and tail. This is done in a specific pattern using pre-selected feathers that are trimmed just right.

We also had to decorate the cages for the Tiki Room. We were given a cage fabricated from metal tubing. We applied Bondo to the tubing (Bondo could easily be carved to look like wood), and then painted and decorated the cages.

We had a wonderful teacher for the whole Tiki project in Leota Thomas. Leota and Harriet Burns were the Imagineers who furred and feathered the original Tiki Birds for Disneyland, and then later for Walt Disney World.

Leota was originally from the Walt Disney Studios, where she had worked in the Ink & Paint Department. She came over to WED when Disney first started the company. Without this wonderful lady teaching us the intricacies of the Tiki Birds, it would have been very time-consuming to figure out the exact method. She also taught us the use of 'Animal Vinyl Paint', which was used on the flexible bodies of the Animatronic figures, animal and human, as well as the Elephants, Hippos and others in the Jungle Cruise. The paint was actually a liquid form of the skin itself."

START WITH THE JUNGLE

Want to see one of the very first sections of Disneyland ever created and which still exists today? Then head over to the Jungle Cruise and hop aboard a boat for a voyage into the past.

As a master story-teller, Walt Disney knew that the foliage of the Jungle Cruise was paramount to creating a believable jungle experience. Small, recently planted trees, bushes and shrubs separated by bare soil would not provide the experience or story Walt wanted to give his guests as they journeyed deep into the jungle. He wanted it to be lush, green and thick with plants large and small. In order to create such a landscape, he knew all of the seeds and foliage would need to be planted a year in advance of the park's opening day in July, 1955, as this would give the plants an entire growing season before guests journeyed the attraction's winding rivers. To that end, he charged the firm of Evans and Reeves with the task, stating..."*In this corner of Disneyland there will be a jungle. Grow a jungle. It has to look like the Tropics and like deepest Africa, and like Australia and Asia and the Amazon.*"

This makes the Jungle Cruise one of the oldest attractions in the park.

Fun Fact: There are over 500 varieties of trees at Disneyland, including one from each continent, except Antarctica.

A MICKEY MOUSE PLANT???

Scientific Name: Ochna serrulata
Common Name: Mickey Mouse Plant

The Jungle Cruise attraction takes guests for a journey down the major rivers of Africa, Asia and South America amidst a dense, green and overgrown jungle. In order to provide a realistic experience for his guests, Walt sent Disney Imagineer and expert horticulturist Bill Evans to gather indigenous seeds and plants from these continents and bring them back to Disneyland with enough time to get established, grow and fill in the attraction by opening day. One of the plants he brought back from South Africa was *Ochna serrulata*, also known as the Mickey Mouse Plant. It's so named because of the configuration of the plant's bright red sepals and the way its black "ears" sometimes form an image of Mickey Mouse!

You can find a Mickey Mouse plant today in a large planter area outside the main door of The World of Disney store in Downtown Disney. Hopefully, it will be in bloom when you find it.

THE DISNEYLAND ROSE

The official rose of Disneyland? Why, it's the "Disneyland Floribunda Rose", of course, and you can buy one for your own yard. They are sold online by Jackson & Perkins, (www.JacksonandPerkins.com) or perhaps at your local garden center.

Look for the Disneyland Rose throughout Disneyland, showcasing petals of orange and pink.

Photo courtesy of Jackson and Perkins

Where Are All The Animals?

Originally, Walt Disney wanted the Jungle Cruise to be an authentic experience, complete with real animals. However, upon further reflection, Walt and his team realized that not only would animals be

unpredictable in their behavior, but they tend to sleep during the day, which means guests on the attraction would probably not be able to see them as Walt intended. The fix?...Disney Imagineers used hydraulics to give motion to realistic looking animal figures, thus being able to control the "animals'" and have them appear active all throughout the day, every day.

Note: It's easy to think Disney Imagineers used Walt's Audio Animatronic technology back in 1955, but this was first used in the Enchanted Tiki Room attraction in 1963, nearly seven years after Disneyland welcomed its first guests.

A Model Cast Member

As guests round the last bend of the Jungle Cruise, they'll notice "Trader Sam" off to the left. Holding a shrunken head, he's offering a special deal...he'll trade two of his heads for only one of yours. "Trader Sam" is actually modeled after a real person, Golden Globe winner, decathlete and football star Woody Strode. In 1954, as Disneyland was being built, Woody was asked by Harper Goff, who

oversaw the construction of the Jungle Cruise, to pose as a model for what became "Trader Sam," as well as other characters in the park.

A TRIBUTE TO HARPER GOFF

Across from the entrance to the Jungle Cruise attraction, you'll spot a window honoring Art Director and Disney Legend, Harper Goff. It reads...

Oriental Tattooing
By Prof. Harper Goff
Banjo Lessons

Harper Goff, along with landscaper Bill Evans, is credited with developing and refining the concept of the Jungle Cruise, one of Disneyland's opening day attractions. Leveraging the award-winning designs he developed for Disney's 1954 live-action film, *20,000 Leagues Under the Sea*, and combining this with inspiration he drew from the 1951 movie, *The African Queen*, Harper brought to Disneyland the thrill-seeking adventure of plying the world's most dangerous jungle rivers.

In addition to being an Art Director, Harper was a skilled banjoist, playing alongside fellow Disney Legend Ward Kimball and other Disney employees in the seven-piece Dixieland band called Firehouse Five Plus Two.

A WEE HOME IN DISNEYLAND

Wouldn't you like to wake up every morning, walk out your front door and step right into Disneyland? For one man, this happens every day.

Make your way to the sign for the Indiana Jones Adventure attraction and study the base of one of the nearby trees, behind a short fence. There you will find the tiny home of Patrick Begorra, the leprechaun who gave permission for Mickey Mouse, Donald Duck, Goofy and Pluto to build Disneyland on the site of his orange grove, as told in the 1955 Golden Book, *Little Man of Disneyland*. In exchange for granting his permission, Patrick asked to have a new home built "out of sight, hidden away" in Disneyland. Mickey Mouse, and no doubt Walt, agreed, and today Patrick can be found "keeping an eye on the place" from this small home in Adventureland.

1955 First Edition printing of Little Man of Disneyland
Author's Personal Collection

ALADDIN'S OTHER LAMP

This next secret promises great wisdom and a look into your future, all for a minor pittance. Tucked into a small alcove at the back of the Bazaar in Adventureland is "Aladdin's Other Lamp."

"Whosoever rubs the lamp (and places coins in the slot below) shall receive the wisdom of the GENIE and have their future revealed."

It's a whimsical interaction with Aladdin's other lamp as it reveals your future in a series of silly jokes and predictions, all with a delightful finish.

COL. NEDLEY LOSTMORE

Located nearby is another sage providing advice, as well as a unique Disneyland souvenir many guests aren't aware exists. Residing in a tiki-adorned kiosk within the South Sea Traders shop is the shrunken head of British explorer, Col. Nedley Lostmore, affectionately known as "Shrunken Ned". As the "Head Shrink of the Jungle", he will dispense a personal diagnosis, along with a souvenir prescription card, for only a

pittance. Insert your coins and receive advice you'll treasure your whole life...if you live that long.

A Nod to the Swiss Family Treehouse

In June of 1999, Disney Imagineers unveiled the new Tarzan's Treehouse. A reflection of Disney's new movie at the time, *Tarzan*, it takes guests on a winding journey through Tarzan's jungle home...an 80' tall tree! Unknown to many, especially those under 20 years of age, is that this attraction replaced one quite similar, the Swiss Family Treehouse. In 1960, Disney released the movie Swiss Family Robinson, a tale about a family shipwrecked on a deserted island, where they built a home from supplies salvaged from their ship and engaged in daily adventures, including battling with pirates. The film was such a success that Disney opened the Swiss Family Treehouse attraction in 1962. Here, as with Tarzan's Treehouse, guests climbed through the tree the Swiss family used as their home.

As with other "new" attractions in Disneyland, Disney Imagineers have paid tribute to the former Swiss Family Treehouse within Tarzan's Treehouse in a number of small ways, the most prominent of which is the upbeat Swisskapolka song, a tune from the 1960 Swiss Family Robinson movie. If you stop and listen carefully, you can hear it playing faintly on the large old phonograph located at the base of the tree at the end of the attraction.

A Hidden
Beauty and the Beast

Look closely for this next secret and you'll be rewarded with a fun reference to Disney's animated hit, *Beauty and the Beast*. After you've descended from Tarzan's Treehouse, peruse the camp at the base of the tree and look for Mrs. Potts and Chip, the teapot and teacup.

It All Finished With A Mouse?

Nearby you'll find a short tree stump. Peer into one of the two "holes" in the side of the stump and you'll find a small critter hidden inside staring back at you. Now look into the hole on the opposite side. Do you dare reach in?

A Towering Perspective of Disneyland

Don't make the mistake of dismissing Tarzan's Treehouse as simply a walk-through attraction, as it reveals an all new perspective of Disneyland.

Make your way up the stairs and high into the branches. There you will find unique aerial views and new perspectives of the Haunted Mansion, Tom Sawyer Island, Splash Mountain and Adventureland, which you cannot get from anywhere else in the park.

Note: Believe it or not, but the tree you wander through actually has a scientific name... *Disneydendron semperflorens grandis*, which means "Large ever-blooming Disney tree."

Indiana Jones Adventure

If the Mercedes-Benz truck at the entrance to the Indiana Jones Adventure queue looks familiar, it should. That's an actual prop from the movie *Raiders of the Lost Ark.* While it is adorned with the same license plate as the truck used in the harrowing desert chase scene of the film, there are a few minor differences.

"Ceiling" Your Fate

As you make your way through the long darkened queue for Indiana Jones Adventure, you'll come to a passageway in which sharpened iron spikes hang from the ceiling threatening to impale you and everyone in your party. On your left is a large somewhat curved cane of bamboo standing vertically. Give it a good solid push (and I mean a *solid* push) and watch as the spiked ceiling begins to lower, sealing your fate.

Give it a Good Tug

As you continue on, you'll come across a large deep chamber with an immense cap stone suspended above it. Perched on the rim of the chamber is a sign which reads, "Caution - Do Not Pull Rope! Handling Fragile Artifacts." The rope is attached to an archaeologist working below who will be quite upset if you pull it. Go ahead...give it a good tug and see what happens.

(Pull hard!)

Eeyore Parked In the Back

Now make your way further along the queue for a secret which will require the assistance of a Cast Member.

The Indiana Jones Adventure attraction was built upon part of the old Eeyore parking lot. As a reminder of this old lot, Disney Imagineers hid one of the Eeyore parking lot signs in the queue. It's very difficult to find, so as you approach the front of the "projector room" in the queue, ask the attending Cast Member to show you the hidden Eeyore parking lot sign. Using a flashlight, they will point to the sign, which is up near the roof at the back of the room, behind the projector. If the Cast Member knows his or her stuff, they'll also point out a fun Hidden Mickey, which is nearby.

Rough Around the Edges

Stepping back into Adventureland, pause for a moment and take notice of the changes which have subtly occurred since you've traveled from Main Street, U.S.A. Here Disney Imagineers have replaced the level brick walkways and crisp curbs defining the streets and pathways with rough-edged pavement disappearing into the undergrowth, and instead of the finely pruned trees and shrubs of the central plaza, the jungle appears to be overgrown and unruly...perfect for an adventure!

INDIANA JONES...SINCE 1896?

That large palm tree right next to the entrance to the Indiana Jones Fastpass station? It's called the Dominguez Palm and, believe it or not, it's well over 100 years old!

Prior to Disneyland being built, 17 different families owned the property upon which Disneyland sits today. One of those families, the Dominguez family, sold their 10 acres to Walt Disney with the condition that the large Canary Island Date Palm planted on their property as a wedding gift in 1896 was not to be removed, but instead it must remain on the property and forever be cared for. Today this tree is revered by Disneyland horticulturists and resides as a treasured element of Adventureland.

Jungle Cruise, 1958 - Photo courtesy of David Eppen

Note: Here's a tip on how to get the perfect photo of the Dominguez Palm, one which isn't of just its trunk surrounded by bamboo. Simply board the Jungle Cruise and take a photo of the tree from the dock, just as you're arriving back at civilization and disembarking your boat.

CHAPTER FOUR

SECRETS OF
NEW ORLEANS SQUARE

"To all who come to Disneyland; welcome. Here age relives fond memories of the past...and here youth may savor the challenge and promise of the future."

– Walt Disney

OPENING DAY
SPEECH IN MORSE CODE

Now make your way across the park to the New Orleans Disneyland Railroad Station and listen for this next secret. Standing at the boarding platform, you'll hear the sound of a telegraph filling

the air, and if you look closely, you'll spot where its coming from, an antique telegraph relay sounder set on the exterior sill of the ticket window of the station. As part of the Disneyland story, someone is inside tapping out an adaptation of Walt Disney's opening day speech in Morse Code welcoming guests young and old to Disneyland.

DECODING THE
DISNEYLAND TELEGRAPH

The following article was written by Mr. George Eldridge and is reprinted with his permission. While it is available elsewhere, I wanted to include it here because it is such a great story about how a Disneyland guest came to have a permanent role in a storied Disneyland attraction quite by accident...

Several years ago I was standing at the New Orleans Train Station at Disneyland Park in Anaheim, California. Echoing in my ears was the sound of a telegraph. I, like every other ham that has visited Disneyland, listened intently to the clicks and clacks and tried to decode the message that was coming from the telegraph sounder. As a practiced CW operator on the ham bands, my first thought was that it wouldn't be too hard to decode the content. Rather than listening for tones, I'd have to think in terms of the electromagnetic sounder, which produced a "click" when energized and a "clack" when released. Thus a dit (dot) would be "click clack" and a dah (dash) would be "click (pause) clack." This sounded good in theory, but in practice it was a little more difficult than I expected. My CW gray matter just hasn't been trained for listening to the clicks and clacks in place of tones! And another thing concerned me: The rhythm of the elements wasn't quite right. In particular, I could hear a "click (pause) clack" that was much longer than the rest. At that moment I decided to return with a tape recorder and investigate further. I wasn't going to stop until I had successfully decoded the message!

A Little Detective Work

When I got home I searched the Internet for any reference to the Disneyland telegraph message. I found one reference that claimed the message was Walt Disney's inaugural speech, given at the opening of Disneyland in 1955. The telegraph message repeated every 49 seconds, however, and even at 25 words per minute it would be about 20 words, so I didn't think it could be the whole speech. As a Disneyland annual pass-holder who lives only 12 miles from the theme park, it wasn't long before I returned with a tape recorder. Actually, it was the evening of Friday, September 5, 1997. I taped about five minutes of the "code" while enduring strange looks from the other guests who were waiting for the train. I took my recorder and headed home to start the task of decoding the message.

The first thing I did was to play the tape at half speed. This made it much easier to hear the clicks and clacks. It also made it easier to hear code elements that didn't correspond to Morse code (at least the Morse code that we use as hams). I remembered seeing a table in the Callbook that listed various telegraph codes. I opened up the Callbook and, sure enough, the Continental Code (used in ham radio) was listed next to the Morse Code (used on land lines in the United States and Canada). I was surprised by the differences between the two!

The letters C, F, J, L, O, P, Q, R, X, Y and Z are different. The figures and punctuation marks are different. And the elements C, O, R, Y and Z are composed of dots and spaces. T is a short dash and L is a longer dash. No wonder I was having trouble decoding the message!

At this point I decided to enlist the aid of my computer. I played the tape into my computer's sound card and digitized the audio. I could then display the waveform and see the clicks and clacks. This was much closer to Samuel F. B. Morse's original telegraph. Morse's original invention had a clockwork that moved a paper tape. The electromagnet pressed a pencil against the tape, making a sequence of dots and dashes on the moving tape. The paper tape was visually decoded to decipher the message. Telegraph operators soon found that they could decode the message just from the sounds, however, so the paper tape became an instant antique. I soon had the message decoded: "WHO COME TO THIS HAPPY PLACE, WELCOME. HERE AGE RELIVES FOND MEMORIES OF THE PAST, AND HERE YOUTH MAY SAVOR THE CHALL" The message repeated with what sounded like a splice between the "CHALL" and "WHO". Did the message start with "ALL WHO" and end with "CH", or did it start with "WHO" and end with "CHALL"? Obviously, there was a problem with the message.

A Call to the Magic Kingdom

I called Disneyland and asked to speak with someone about the damaged message. I was afraid that I might get a brush-off, but the Disney staffers were courteous and did their best to locate someone who could help me. When it became clear that no one at Disneyland could help me, they referred me to the WED studios in Burbank. I called WED and was routed to the media department - the folks there handle the sound effects at the park. I left a message explaining the damaged telegraph message. A couple of days later I received a call from media engineer Glenn Barker. Glenn explained that Disneyland is very serious about keeping things correct

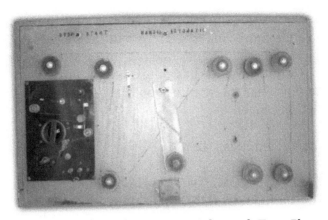

Original Frontierland RR Station Telegraph Tape Player
Photo used with permission
(Though I'm not supposed to reveal from whom!)

and was interested in getting the message fixed. He guessed that the message was accidentally truncated when it was moved from an endless loop tape player to the solid-state digital player used today. I surmised that the media engineer had listened for a repeat in the pattern and keyed in on the distinctive "LL" combination. Unfortunately, he failed to realize that the pattern "LL" occurred twice in the message. Glenn said he'd try to dig up the original tape and call me back. A couple of weeks later I got a call from Glenn saying he had found the original tape - but there was a problem. On the original tape the message repeats several times, but because Glenn didn't understand telegraphy, he couldn't tell where the message started or ended. I offered to decode the message and mark the beginning and end points. Glenn played the tape into my voice mail, which I downloaded onto my computer and decoded as before. I edited the sound clip so it contained just one copy of the message and played the clip into Glenn's voice mail. Glenn was able to update the digital player at the New Orleans Train Station so that it plays the correct message. He even added a pause at the end of the message to make the repeat more obvious.

It's interesting that we used modern technology to send and decode a telegraph message. I'm sure Samuel Morse never expected that someone would one day use a computer to decode a telegraph message. I had achieved my goal of decoding the message and had an interesting adventure in doing it. I hope my tale has entertained you enough that the next time you hear telegraphy you'll make an effort to decode the hidden message.

And the corrected message?...

"TO ALL WHO COME TO THIS HAPPY PLACE, WELCOME. HERE AGE RELIVES FOND MEMORIES OF THE PAST, AND HERE YOUTH MAY SAVOR THE CHALLENGE AND PROMISE OF THE FUTURE."

A DEPOT SO
DEAR TO MY HEART

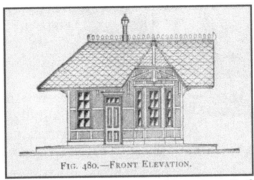

FIG. 480.—FRONT ELEVATION.

From "Buildings and Structures of American Railroads"
Walter G. Berg

For many guests, the Disneyland Railroad New Orleans Square Station is just a quaint prop, perhaps nothing more than an overlooked backdrop to New Orleans Square. Little do they know the station plays a starring role in an interesting story of Disney history reaching back to the late 1800s.

In 1949, Walt Disney released the motion picture "So Dear to My Heart", and as part of this film, he wanted to include a train depot which captured the essence of small-town America. Walt asked Ward Kimball, a Disney Imagineer and years later a Disney Legend, if he had any suggestions for a design which he could use to build a train depot as a prop in the film. Ward grabbed an "old book" of his (*Buildings and Structures of American Railroads* by Walter G. Berg - 1893) off a shelf and showed Walt a drawing for a "Flag Stop" depot used on the Pottsville Branch of the Lehigh Valley Railroad in the late 1800s, which he thought would work well. Walt agreed and had his Art Director and Set Designers use the drawing as a reference in building the depot. After Walt had finished filming "So Dear to My Heart", he offered the train depot prop to Ward who, like Walt, was a large-scale model railroad enthusiast. Ward had built a railroad in his backyard and both Walt and Ward thought the depot would make an excellent addition. It took a lot of work on Ward's part to convert the

incomplete movie prop into a sound structure, but soon Ward had a new train depot, which he called "Grizzly Flats."

In turn, Walt Disney used the Grizzly Flats depot Ward Kimball had so skillfully built as the template for the Disneyland Railroad New Orleans Square Station you see today.

Tip: For fans of Walt Disney, Disneyland railroading and Ward Kimball, I highly recommend three compelling resources. The first is the outstanding book, titled *Walt Disney's Railroad Story*, by Michael Broggie, the son of Disney Legend Roger Broggie. This is perhaps one of the finest books I've read regarding this important element in the history of Walt Disney, as well as the theme parks. The second is a seven-part video available on YouTube, which features an interview of Ward Kimball by Tom Snyder at Ward's Grizzly Flats. And the third is *Welcome Aboard The Disneyland Railroad! - The Complete History in Words and Pictures - Collector's Edition*, by Disneyland Railroad historian Steve DeGaetano.

"NOTE" DISNEY'S ATTENTION TO DETAIL

Disney's attention to detail in its storytelling is legendary, and here's another fine and always overlooked example. You won't get close enough to read it with the naked eye, but if you use your camera you'll spot it. Take a photo of the luggage stacked at the Disneyland Railroad New Orleans Square Station, and if you zoom in and study it close enough, you'll spot a small round luggage sticker for the Preservation Hall Jazz Band, an homage to the famed band known for its performing of outstanding New Orleans-style jazz in the French Quarter since 1961, just a few years after Disneyland opened.

LaFitte's Anchor

If you make your way over by the Rivers of America, you'll no doubt find LaFitte's Anchor, believed to be over 250 years old and quite possibly from a pirate ship Jean LaFitte sailed in the Gulf of Mexico. According to the affixed bronze plaque, it is...

"Said to be from a pirate ship commanded by Jean LaFitte in the battle of New Orleans, January 8, 1815. It is also said that LaFitte's privateering ships left a wake of blood from the mainland to Barataria Bay." The plaque finishes with...*"But don't believe everything you read."*

In the year before Disneyland opened, Imagineers scoured the country looking for antiques to use as props within the park, and they found LaFitte's anchor in an antique shop in New Orleans...near the Gulf of Mexico.

Note: Did you notice the sign hanging above when you boarded your boat on the Pirates of the Caribbean attraction? It reads "Laffite's Landing". Observant guests will notice the two different spellings of Laffite's name.

THE HAUNTED MANSION

Those souls who visit the Haunted Mansion when it's crowded are entombed in a queue line which seems to stretch for an eternity. However, all is not lost as the line winds its way past a couple of secrets all the other mortal souls miss when they walk straight up the front walkway to the mansion.

As the queue line begins over by the Disneyland Railroad Train Station in New Orleans Square, guests are treated to a collection of silly crypt names, including Theo Later, Ray N. Carnation, I.L. Beback, U.R. Gone and more before passing by the first of two pet cemeteries. (Yes, unknown to most, there are two pet cemeteries.) As guests approach the entrance, they are reminded of life's fragile nature by the presence of an old horse-drawn hearse, pulled by a horse which has perhaps already gone on to the "other side." Pause here long enough, and you'll hear it call out with a hearty neigh from wherever it now resides.

RESERVATIONS ACCEPTED

Approach the hearse and you'll find a sign inside which reads...

"Reservations Accepted – Ghost Relations Department – Disneyland – Please Do Not Apply in Person!"

THE SECRET
SECOND PET CEMETERY

Unless guests know where to look when exiting the Haunted Mansion, there's not a ghost of a chance they'll see this next secret...a second pet cemetery hidden away on the north side of the Haunted Mansion.

In the early 1980s, Disney Imagineer Kim Irvine, daughter of Leota Toombs Thomas, had the idea of using the rarely-seen side lawn of Disneyland's Haunted Mansion as a pet cemetery. Using off-the-shelf statuary, she worked with fellow Imagineer Chris Goosman to adorn each tombstone with witty epitaphs for such beloved pets as "Miss Kitty", "Bully" and "Big Jake", the dog seen in the photo above. This new addition proved to be very popular with guests, so much so that Walt Disney Imagineering decided to add a larger pet cemetery in the front yard of the Haunted Mansion in 1993, where it has been light-heartedly haunting guests ever since.

When exiting the Haunted Mansion, look for a small walkway which heads along the north wall of the building. There, just beyond the shrubbery, is the second pet cemetery containing the beloved pets of the ghosts of the Haunted Mansion.

FOUND HANGING
IN THE PORTRAIT CHAMBER

Believe it or not, but the wallpaper found hanging in the haunting portrait chamber can be owned by mere mortals. Guests can purchase this very same wallpaper for their own homes through Bradbury & Bradbury Art Wallpapers. The collection is called "Dresser II Roomset – Lily".

HAVING A BALL
WITH MADAME LEOTA

As you make your way into The Séance Circle, you'll spot the disembodied head of Madame Leota floating in a crystal ball. The face you see is that of Leota Toombs Thomas, a Disney Imagineer who was extremely talented in developing and artfully applying the finishing touches of the skin, fur and feathers on attraction figures, including the animals for The Jungle Cruise, the birds of The Enchanted Tiki Room, and the ghosts of the Haunted Mansion.

According to 30 year Imagineer Cindy Bothner, whom worked with and trained under Leota Toombs Thomas, she was a very sweet woman with a soft spoken voice, and she considered it to be quite an honor to have her visage featured in a scene within a Disneyland attraction.

Note that while Madame Leota's head in the Séance Circle is voiced by Disney voice talent Eleanor Audley, the small

"Little Leota" bride featured at the end of the ride, the one which beckons guests to "Huuurry baaaack", features both the face and voice of Leota Toombs Thomas.

"Serpents and spiders, tail of a rat...call in the spirits, wherever they're at. Rap on a table, it's time to respond...send us a message from somewhere beyond! Goblins and ghoulies from last Halloween...awaken the spirits with your tambourine. Creepies and crawlies, toads in a pond...let there be music from regions beyond. Wizards and witches, wherever you dwell...give us a hint by ringing a bell."

SECRETS OF THE ATTIC

The following is an article written by Jeff Baham, the host of www.DoomBuggies.com and author of the outstanding book, The Unauthorized Story of Walt Disney's Haunted Mansion. *My thanks to Jeff for writing about this secret for my book.*

Perhaps you've taken a tour of Disneyland's home to 999 happy haunts, the Haunted Mansion. For an unoccupied house it's certainly a lively place, with rattling doorknobs, a séance in full swing, and a swinging wake welcoming mourners to dance until morning, which never seems to arrive. But at the top of the house, there's that musty attic, filled with mysteries that leave many guests scratching their heads. After all, most people's attics are dank, dusty places with the occasional neglected baby carriage or a few boxes of old toys strewn about. The Haunted Mansion's attic, however, contains numerous well-designed vignettes celebrating the various weddings of a young bride, named Constance Hatchaway, to a number of unlucky suitors, all of whom are shown to have literally lost their heads after hitching themselves to this black widow of a bride.

But the Haunted Mansion attic wasn't always this way. In fact, most guests don't realize this, but in its earliest incarnation, the Haunted Mansion's attic was probably more like yours or mine: dusty, empty; a dark void with cobwebs hanging down from the rafters that would brush disturbingly against the riders' faces as they traveled through the shadows in silence, save for the ominous echo of a lonely heartbeat.

After entering the dark, sparsely outfitted attic, guests would encounter the bride to their left; a ghostly apparition far more menacing than the current character who speaks with a wink. The original bride would simply glare with glowing eyes through a decrepit visage, her transparent wedding gown draped over her body as she slowly raised a flickering candle up toward her blackened, skeletal face.

Credit Disney Imagineer Ken Anderson with coming up with the idea of hosting a wedding in the Haunted Mansion and establishing the idea of a bride inhabiting the place. That original bride was eventually based on the designs of Imagineer Marc Davis, who created many concepts for the character, which ranged from the silly to the sublime.

But the bride was not the only character Davis intended for that attic. After glimpsing the bride, across the track to the viewers' right, another ghost would come into view. This ghost, hoisting a hat box in his hand, would become legendary as he was only in place in the Haunted Mansion for weeks at most. But this character, another decrepit ghost with a transparent cloak and a top hat on his head, was designed as an obvious companion to the lone bride. Leaning on a shaky cane, this "Hat Box Ghost" would glare at you with an evil grin as his head disappeared from his body in time with the bride's heartbeat, and would then reappear in the hat box.

Well, his head would reappear in theory, that is. In real life, the special effect didn't work so well - perhaps because the carriages by which viewers tour the attic were too close to the character to make the lighting effect work. Davis decided his character wasn't creating the desired effect and had it removed shortly after the character was installed - though the legendary character lives on through Disney merchandise, Disney marketing and, most importantly, in the imagination of the Haunted Mansion's legion of fans.

In fact, it's said that the Hat Box Ghost still prowls the attic of the Haunted Mansion to this day. Have YOU seen him? Take a closer look the next time you ride through that old mansion. It may be that he never really left his home, after all...

A HIDDEN WALT

As you wander the streets of New Orleans Square, stop in at the Crystal d'Orleans shop to discover a truly unique portrait of Walt Disney.

There, above the fine crystal and set into a frame, is a reflective disc with a smiling image of Walt brushed into the center.

Club 33

There it is...right next door to the Blue Bayou Restaurant in New Orleans Square. A simple, nondescript door with an address of "33 Royal St." To most guests, it's just another door, passed by without a second thought, but to those in the know, it's the *former* entrance to "Club 33", Walt Disney's exclusive "members only" club and restaurant for V.I.P.s and dignitaries. Celebrities, Disney executives, V.I.P.s and even regular Disneyland guests can wait years to join, and it all comes with an expensive initiation fee, but those who are welcomed as members receive unique dining and membership benefits in an exclusive Disneyland setting.

A Mast See

Disney Imagineers are masters at storytelling. With the addition of a single visual element, they can enhance an existing storyline, as well as expand the boundaries of both Disneyland...and your imagination.

New Orleans Square is set in the early 19th century port city of New Orleans, yet many guests miss seeing the tall masts of the ship docked nearby. Stand either on the edge of The Rivers of America, opposite Orleans

Street, or out a ways from the entrance to The Pirates of the Caribbean attraction and look up above the buildings of New Orleans Square. There, in the distance above the rooftops, are the sails of a three-masted ship unloading cargo and taking on supplies.

A PIRATE'S FORTUNE

Now make your way over towards the Pieces of Eight gift shop and step into a darkened gated passageway where you'll find the fortune-telling pirate, Fortune Red. Housed in a coin-operated booth, Fortune Red dispenses your fortune for a mere pittance. What he won't tell you is how that Disneyland map you have in your hands is tied to the one in his. The pirate's treasure map he's holding is an original illustration drawn by Sam McKim, a Disney Legend who was responsible for creating many  Disneyland illustrations, including the prized Disneyland souvenir maps issued between 1958 and 1964.

THE IMAGINEER'S ATTENTION TO HISTORICAL DETAIL

As you step out of the Pieces of Eight gift shop, take a look under the balcony across the street. There, up and out of the way and easily overlooked, is a small "Fire Mark" with the words "Disneyland Fire Dept." underneath.

In another display of the Imagineers' attention to accurate historical detail, this fire mark reflects the state of fire protection services available to property owners in America at the turn of the 20th century. Building owners would purchase fire insurance and, in turn, receive a fire mark such as this made of lead or cast iron, which they affixed to the exterior of their building between the first and second story. In the event of a fire, one or more volunteer fire departments would extinguish the fire and, in turn, bill the insurance company indicated on the fire mark for their services.

In this case, the building owner has subscribed to the fire protection services of the Disneyland Fire Department and received the corresponding fire mark.

Can you find any other plaques in New Orleans Square?

Note: The fire marks shown here are historically accurate, with the first being modeled after a mark created by the Associated Firemen's Insurance Company of Baltimore in 1848, and the second created by the United Fireman's Insurance Company of Philadelphia, though this featured a "U" and "F" on the face, instead of a "D" and "L".

A Golden Tribute
to Walt and Roy

Now find the nearby Cafe Orleans and take notice of the wrought iron scroll work of the railings overhead. Notice the gold initials woven into the pattern? This artwork pays homage to Walt Disney and his brother, Roy Disney.

CHAPTER FIVE

SECRETS OF FRONTIERLAND

"All of us have a cause to be proud of our country's history, shaped by the pioneering spirit of our forefathers...Our adventures are designed to give you the feeling of having lived, even for a short while, during our country's pioneer days."
- Walt Disney

13 Flags

Passing into Frontierland from the Central Plaza, you'll enter into the old Log Fort. Stop for a moment and try to find all 13 of the small flags atop the stockade. Some are out in the open, while others are difficult to spot in the trees. These flags represent those carried by American troops during the Revolutionary War, a period when the United States had not yet adopted a single flag for our country.

It was on June 14, 1777, when Congress approved our official national flag, The Stars and Stripes.

Original 1955 Lanterns

To your left is the Pioneer Mercantile, a trading post supplying western wear, leather goods, precious stones and all kinds of Disneyland souvenirs, including Mickey Mouse ears, for those who are about to venture out yonder into the Wild West.

As you step onto the porch at the entrance of the Pioneer Mercantile, look up and you will notice a collection of lanterns hanging from a couple of large wooden beams. The red lanterns are just "modern day" decorations, but the six green lanterns hanging here are a piece of historical Disneyland, as these are the actual Deitz and Embury lanterns which the Imagineers hung in Frontierland during Disneyland's opening year in 1955.

CROCKETT & RUSSEL HAT CO.

As you make your way through Frontierland, you'll notice the building façade adorned with the large lettering "Crockett & Russel Hat Co.", as well as a window which recognizes actor Fess Parker, reading "Davy Crockett - Coonskin Cap Supply Co."

This entire building façade pays homage to Fess Parker and Buddy Epsen, two actors who, in 1954 and 1955, starred in three one-hour television episodes as Davy Crockett and his friend, George Russel, as they made their way through the wild frontier while rafting down rivers, camping in the woods, and even fighting a bear. The adventures of the two instantly captured the imagination of children all across the country, especially young boys, and overnight the show became a nationwide sensation, the likes of which had never been seen before, thanks to the power of television. The show's theme song, "The Ballad of Davy Crockett" shot to #1 on the charts and held that position for three months in a row, and, catching Disney by surprise, it seemed every child in America was soon sporting a buckskin coat, a frontier rifle and a coonskin cap.

Sounds Like Fireworks

Over by the Golden Horse Saloon, beyond the Stage Door Cafe, you'll find a mural for Laod Bhang & Co. Fireworks. (Sound it out) This is an excellent example of Disney Imagineers having some fun in a mural which is often overlooked. You'll also find Laod Bhang referenced in numerous places elsewhere, including a pin trading cart over in Disney California Adventure.

Frontierland Transition

Now look directly across from the Laod Bhang Fireworks & Co. mural, on the other side of the seating area for the Stage Door Cafe and River Belle Terrace, and you'll spot two railings which meet atop a low brick wall, right next to the main walkway. One railing is made of wood, while the other is made of wrought iron, and between the two is a small planter. It's subtle, but this marks the spot where Frontierland ends and New Orleans Square begins.

THE DAWN REDWOOD

Standing right next to The Golden Horseshoe, facing towards New Orleans Square, is a rare Dawn Redwood. This tree was thought to be extinct for 1.5 million years, until it was discovered growing in China in 1943. Bill Evans, the man Walt Disney charged with landscaping Disneyland, was given one of four cuttings from the newly discovered tree, which he cultivated and ultimately planted at Disneyland, where it continues to grow today.

Note: Unlike the California Redwood, the Dawn Redwood is deciduous and loses its needles in the winter.

MARK TWAIN RIVERBOAT

Here's another fun secret so many guests walk right past, one which provides an exciting new way to see part of Disneyland, much like the Omnibus does with Main Street, U.S.A. Board the Mark Twain Riverboat and find a place on the front railing of the top deck. From here, you'll see The Haunted Mansion, Splash Mountain, Big Thunder Mountain Railroad, Tom Sawyer Island, New Orleans Square, the Matterhorn and more from an entirely new and moving perspective.

A Unique Disneyland Souvenir

This next secret will pay off with a unique V.I.P. Disneyland experience few guests ever get to enjoy.

Board the Mark Twain Riverboat and speak with a Cast Member about joining the Captain in the wheelhouse to pilot the riverboat on its journey around Tom Sawyer Island. If the opportunity is available, you'll join the captain, help steer the Mark Twain Riverboat, ring the bell and even pull the cord to blow the steam whistle, all while taking in exciting new views of Disneyland from high atop the Mark Twain Riverboat. And to top it off, when finished, you'll receive a rare souvenir...your very own Mark Twain Riverboat Pilot's Certificate!

Certificate courtesy of Megan Westby

More Forced Perspective

When designing the Mark Twain Riverboat, the Disney Imagineers were faced with a problem. Building the craft to its original dimensions would make it too large and overwhelming for its setting in the park. The answer...forced perspective, the same trick of the eye used with the buildings on Main Street, U.S.A., Sleeping Beauty Castle and the Matterhorn. As a result, the Mark Twain Riverboat is built to a 5/8 scale.

Historical American Flags

This next secret is overlooked by a vast majority of guests, as it is easily lost amidst all the patriotic flags and bunting adorning the Mark Twain Riverboat.

When disembarking the attraction, take note of the different historic flags flying atop the eight flag poles at the entrance. Including the Betsy Ross Flag, the Star Spangled Banner and "Old Glory", these flags and their corresponding plaques explaining their significance convey the dramatic seminal moments in the history of America's flag.

Subtle Transitions

As you make your way throughout Disneyland, notice how the Disney Imagineers have gone to great lengths to transition the story from land to land. Much of the transition takes place with differing architectural elements, as the attractions in Tomorrowland obviously differ from those in Frontierland, but much is also achieved with less noticeable changes in colors, music, landscaping, signs, fonts, foliage, etc. Perhaps one of the most subtle transition elements is themed paving. For example, notice how the red bricks, curbs and clean linear streets of Main Street, U.S.A. differ from the rough surfaces and undefined edges of Adventureland, while the pavement of Frontierland reveals the hoof marks and wheel tracks of an old horse and buggy.

BIG THUNDER
MOUNTAIN RAILROAD

This next secret reveals more about Disneyland's colorful past.

Make your way through the queue of Big Thunder Mountain Railroad and you'll notice a collection of old western buildings on the hill. What most guests don't realize is that these very buildings first had a home as the small mining town of Rainbow Ridge in an early attraction at Disneyland. It was here guests boarded the old Mine Train Through Nature's Wonderland, a slow-moving train which journeyed through Beaver Valley, Bear Country, the Living Desert and Rainbow Caverns while showcasing the story of America's wilderness. Towering geysers, rushing waterfalls, brown bears fishing for a meal, desert landscapes with perilous balancing rocks and more all provided a view into America's great untamed West. After opening in 1960, the attraction ran for 17 years before closing in 1977 to make room for an exciting new attraction...Big Thunder Mountain Railroad!

Today you can still see a remnant of the original Mine Train Through Nature's Wonderland attraction. As you exit Big Thunder Mountain Railroad, look directly across the pathway and you'll spot an abandoned railway tunnel. Though all boarded up, it leads directly to Disneyland's history.

A Tribute to Walt and 1955 Disneyland

Now, just before you begin to climb the set of double stairs leading to the boarding platform, look to your right and you'll find a hanging lantern with a distinct "Dietz" logo on the glass globe.

In 1955, when Walt was building Disneyland, he bought all of the lanterns used in Frontierland from the R.E. Dietz Lantern Co., a manufacturer of lanterns used all across the American frontier, as well as throughout its railroads. Typically, the Imagineers do not allow for the display of "outside company" logos within the park, save for exceptions involving sponsorship. In this case, however, this distinctive logo placement is a nod to Walt and the year Disneyland opened. Unfortunately, the original 1955 lanterns were replaced because their original tin components wore out over time.

A Tribute to Tony Wayne Baxter

Hidden throughout Big Thunder Mountain Railroad at Disneyland, and every park where this attraction exists, is a clever tribute to the Disney Imagineer credited with its creation. Located on the Builders Plates of each locomotive, as well as elsewhere, including an old steam compressor, is a logo which includes the initials "BTM". At first glance, this is clearly a reference to "Big Thunder Mountain". However, if you study the "M", you'll see it looks more like an inverted "W", which it is. Pat Burke, the

Disney Imagineer who acquired all of the antique mining equipment you see all around you from throughout the west, as well as gave the attraction its "rusty" look, purposely created this logo with the "W" upside down, so as to provide a cleverly hidden homage to the attraction's creator, Tony Wayne Baxter.

BIG THUNDER MOUNTAIN
GEO-MARKER

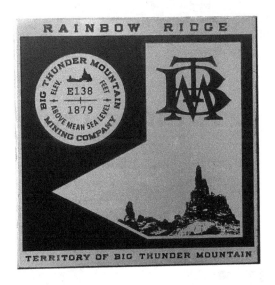

Located on the ground in the middle of the boarding platform on the left-hand side of the Big Thunder Mountain station is an easily overlooked Survey Marker for the attraction. Labeled "Rainbow Ridge – Territory of Big Thunder Mountain", it was placed here in 1879 and indicates an elevation of 138' above mean sea level. Astute guests will recognize this elevation as being the same as that of the Disneyland Railroad Station at the park's entrance.

Even Wilder
Fun in the Wilderness!

Want to make your ride on Big Thunder Mountain even more exciting? Enter the queue and ask a Cast Member if you may sit in the back car of the train where the "wildest ride in the wilderness" is even wilder!

A Huge Hidden Mickey

Just as you begin climbing the hill towards the goat chewing a stick of dynamite, look to your left and find the large gear on the ground with two smaller gears positioned to create an upside down Hidden Mickey.

It's Quittin' Time!

Pass by the town of Rainbow Ridge at Big Thunder Mountain Railroad during the day and you'll notice things are awfully quiet, as the miners are out working in the mines, but at night the town comes alive with lights, noise and music.

WHO KNEW HOODOOS?

The landscape of Big Thunder Mountain Railroad at Disneyland is based upon the hoodoos of Bryce Canyon National Park in Utah, while the landscape of Big Thunder Mountain Railroad at the Magic Kingdom of Walt Disney World in Florida is based upon the cliffs and bluffs of Utah's Monument Valley.

THERE ARE CATS IN DISNEYLAND?

With a bit of irony, Disneyland is patrolled by feral cats! Many years ago, feral cats began to appear at the park, and instead of removing them, Disneyland Cast Members allowed them to remain, since they did an excellent job of eradicating rodents, especially those which gravitate towards the more landscaped areas of Adventureland and Frontierland. A rumor you'll often hear is that Cast Members release hundreds of cats each night to patrol the park, but that isn't the case. (Can you imagine having to herd hundreds of cats each morning before the park opens so you can "release" them again the next night?!") Instead, a small number of cats are monitored, fed and housed at different areas within Disneyland where they "patrol" throughout the day and night.

Note: These cats tend to shy away from the big crowds of the day, but now and again you may spot one amongst the shrubbery of Adventureland, along the Disneyland Railroad line or in Frontierland. Keep an eye out and you may spot one at any of these locations or anywhere else within the park.

THUNDER KITTY

Perhaps the most famous of Disneyland's cats is Thunder Kitty. Named by Cast Members, this gray and white cat can often be found in the queue of Big Thunder Mountain Railroad in the morning lazing in the warm sun. As the day progresses and the park becomes busier, he'll find a more secluded spot to rest.

If you board the Big Thunder Mountain Railroad train on the left side of the boarding platform, look to the right as the train leaves the station and perhaps you will spot a picture in a frame holding open a window. This is a photo taken of Thunder Kitty when he hopped up into a child's stroller to take a nap!

Photo courtesy of Megan Westby

TOM SAWYER ISLAND IN MISSOURI?

There is a long-standing rumor of Tom Sawyer Island officially belonging to the State of Missouri. While absurd as this may sound, it does have a ring of truth to it! According to Dave Smith of the Disney Archives...

"The whole thing about Tom Sawyer Island being part of Missouri came from the opening ceremonies in 1956. Phil Donnelly, the Governor of Missouri, sent a tongue-in-cheek letter to Governor Goodwin Knight of California asking him "to take

appropriate action which will cause the Tom Sawyer Island in Disneyland, California, to be deeded to the Sovereign State of Missouri, the only true and rightful possessor of any and all Tom Sawyer Islands in the world."

A TRUE
DISNEYLAND FISH STORY

For a while after Disneyland opened, the Rivers of America around Tom Sawyer Island were stocked with catfish and river perch, and guests were invited to fish off the dock at Catfish Cove.

SAILING SHIP COLUMBIA

As you make your way around Tom Sawyer Island and the Rivers of America, find the Sailing Ship Columbia, often docked at Fowler's Harbor.

Many of the crafts found in Disneyland are scaled down in size to fit the park, from the 5/8 scale of the Disneyland Fire Engine on Main Street, U.S.A. to the 5/8 scale of the Mark Twain Riverboat. However, the 84-foot tall Columbia Sailing Ship on the Rivers of America is a full-scale replica of the first American ship to circumnavigate the globe. The secret? Board the ship and step below to discover a museum displaying how the crew of the ship lived during their seagoing journeys over 200 years ago.

CRITTER COUNTRY SECRETS

Image courtesy of www.davelandweb.com

Country Bear Jamboree may be long gone, but guests can still find some of their old friends from this classic attraction...if they know *when and where* to look!

Make your way over to The Many Adventures of Winnie the Pooh in Critter Country, hop aboard an oversized beehive, and be on alert. As you slowly wind your way through the attraction, you'll pass through the Heffalumps and Woozles section. Immediately after you leave this section, look UP and behind you and you will see these three beloved characters high on the wall. The Many Adventures of Winnie the Pooh attraction took the place of the Country Bear Jamboree, and this is the Disney Imagineers' homage to not only Max, Buff and Melvin, but to the former attraction as well.

CRITTER COUNTRY
CANDY CRITTERS

After you've made the 5-story drop into the briar patch on Splash Mountain, walk over to the Pooh Corner gift shop and make your way to the back where you'll find in-house confectioners practicing their craft while making your new favorite treats. Candied "Mickey Mouse" apples, chocolate drizzled Tigger Tails, hand-dipped Rice Krispies treats and more are all made with magic right before your eyes!

AN UNDERGROUND SECRET

In one of the better examples of Disney theming extending beyond the attractions, stop in at The Briar Patch gift shop and look up to find you've burrowed underground. There, growing through the roof, are huge carrots and roots!

CHAPTER SIX

SECRETS OF TOMORROWLAND

"Tomorrow can be a wonderful age. Our scientists today are opening the doors of the Space Age to achievements that will benefit our children and generations to come...The Tomorrowland attractions have been designed to give you an opportunity to participate in adventures that are a living blueprint of our future."

- Walt Disney

RIDE IN THE
FRONT OF THE MONORAIL

Want to sit in the very front of the Monorail as it makes its way through Disneyland to the Tomorrowland station, or from Tomorrowland to the Downtown Disney station? You are more than welcome  to. Simply approach a Cast Member at the boarding station of your choice and inform them that you'd like to sit in the pilot's cabin. You'll be boarded at the first available opportunity, which is usually the first or second Monorail to arrive. It's a unique new way for the entire family to see Disneyland.

Please note that the pilot's cabin seats up to four guests.

WALKED FROM THE
PAST INTO THE FUTURE

This next secret is very subtle, but obvious once you notice it.

For Walt it was all about the story, the guest experience, and the creation of the magic. From the berm which surrounds Disneyland to remove any visual references to the outside world, to the memorable music which lifts your spirits as you walk throughout the park, he wanted to ensure guests would get lost in the magic and memories of the story while they are at Disneyland.

Legend has it that one day while Walt was in the park, he noticed a Frontierland Cast Member adorned in western attire walking through Tomorrowland while on his way from costuming to his work station. In other words, the past was walking right through the future and all the guests could see it. While this kind of conduct would've been fine at a lesser park, Walt felt this glaring juxtaposition took away from the magic, so he began a policy where Cast Members of each Land could stay only within their Land while "on stage". Not only is this why you won't see Cast Members from one Land within another as you walk throughout Disneyland, but it was also the inspiration for the underground Utilidors in use at Walt Disney World today.

ALL THE PLANTS ARE EDIBLE?

An often repeated rumor is that all of the plants found in Tomorrowland are edible, but this isn't the case. A more accurate statement is that most of the ephemeral plants planted in the beds throughout Tomorrowland are edible, including kale, artichoke, lettuce, rosemary, parsley and more, while the more permanent plants within the hardscape, such as snake plants, tree ferns, jade plants, etc., are not.

ONLY ONE LETTER... BUT 3,000 MILES...APART

This next secret may not be out of this world, but it is kind of fun to know.

Pay attention and you'll notice Disneyland's "Astro Orbitor" attraction is known by a slightly different name at the Magic Kingdom in Walt Disney World. The difference is one single letter, with Walt Disney World's Magic Kingdom attraction known as the "Astro Orbiter".

Walt Disney World's Astro Orbiter initially opened as the Star

Jets attraction in 1974. It ran for twenty years before closing as part of Tomorrowland's extensive renovation in 1994. Reopening in 1995, the new attraction was renamed the "Astro Orbiter."

Disneyland's version of this attraction opened in July, 1967 as the Rocket Jets. Closing in 1997, it underwent a major renovation patterned after Disneyland Paris' Orbitron attraction, and as such, reopened in 1998 as the new Astro Orbitor.

AN OUT OF THIS WORLD TRIBUTE

Making your way through Hyperspace Mountain's queue, you'll see a sign which reads, "Bay 12 – Command Module – Capt. J. Hench". This is a tribute to Disney Legend John Hench, one of Walt Disney's most talented artists and lead designer for much of Disneyland and its classic attractions, as well as attractions within the Magic Kingdom, including the original roller coaster in the dark, Space Mountain.

SMS-077

As you enter the loading bay for Space Mountain, take note of the "SMS-077" marking on the space craft suspended above. Designating Space Mountain Station 077, this is the Imagineers' nod to Space Mountain's opening day in May of 1977.

A CASE FOR OPENING DAY

There isn't much to see inside HyperSpace Mountain, as it's completely dark and flies by at light speed, but when you step into the gift shop, look for a transport case high on an

overhead shelf, which Disney Imagineers have labeled with a tracking number you may find to be familiar...07171955.

THE ROCKETEER

As you stroll about Tomorrowland, you'll find a popcorn cart with a somewhat rare Disney character turning the crank. Inside is The Rocketeer, from Disney's 1991 film by the same name. In this film, a young pilot from the 1930s becomes a high-flying masked hero after discovering a unique jet pack prototype.

AUTOPIA HISTORY

Of all the attractions in Tomorrowland, perhaps none generates the real-world excitement for those too young to drive as Autopia. Here, young guests get the opportunity to hop

into the front seat of a real car and drive with the top down on a Disneyland freeway.

Anything which moves guests at Disneyland, including the Monorail, the Matterhorn Bobsleds, and the Doombuggies of the Haunted Mansion, was designed by Disney Legend Bob Gurr, and shortly after being hired in 1954, Bob was charged with designing and building Disneyland's new Autopia cars. Following the practices of the automotive industry, Bob first designed the cars on paper, and then, with the assistance of students at the Art Center College of Design in Pasadena, California, progressed to creating a full-sized model of a car out of clay, which is called a "clay buck."

From the clay buck, a mold is then made, which in turn is used to create the final vehicle.

The clay buck was built in the North Hollywood garage of Joe Thompson, one of the teachers at the Art Center College of Design, and after it was finished, Bob needed Walt to approve the design. However, being new to the company, he figured a big, important studio head would never come over to someone's garage, so he asked Walt if he could bring the clay model over to the studio for approval, to which Walt replied, *"You're going to bring that big heavy thing over here just so I can look at it? Nonsense. We can all drive there in a few minutes."* So Roger Broggie, Dick Irvine, Bill Cottrell, Bob and Walt all piled into a car and headed over to the garage. Once there, Walt sat down in the clay buck. Unfortunately, the clay was still sticky, so Walt ended up with it all over his jacket, but he liked Bob's design and approved the car for production.

In the words of Bob Gurr..."*I never saw Walt act like a big-shot. He had high standards of excellence, but he was never demanding. He never wanted people to go out of their way just to serve him. Fact is, he would go out of his way to save time for us, and that made everything go more smoothly.*"

I'd like to thank Disney Legend Bob Gurr and author J. Jeff Kober for this story.

FINDING NEMO SUBMARINE VOYAGE

Now circle around to the Finding Nemo Submarine Voyage, board a sub and peer out your window to find the SCUBA diving mask marked with "P. Sherman – 42 Wallaby Way – Sydney." (You'll need to look quickly!) Those guests with a good memory will recall this as the address repeated constantly by the very forgetful fish, Dory, throughout Disney's 2003 hit movie, "Finding Nemo."

THE GRAND CANYON IN DISNEYLAND?

It may be Tomorrowland, but this secret has to do with yesterday. Its debut on March 31, 1958, to be exact.

It's not shown on your Disneyland map, but board the Disneyland Railroad at the Tomorrowland station and "take a detour" to one of the seven natural wonders of the world. Appearing on your right shortly after you enter a tunnel is one of the largest dioramas ever created, depicting the Grand Canyon. At 306 feet long and 34 feet high, and contained on one seamless canvas, this stunning and historical attraction presents guests with an expansive vista showcasing the canyon's beauty, ever-changing weather and abundant wildlife, including mountain lions, wild turkeys, deer, skunks, snakes and more as they traverse their desert terrain.

Even Further Back in Time

Yes, there are dinosaurs in Disneyland!

As you continue along your journey on the Disneyland Railroad, you'll pass from the Grand Canyon and into the Primeval World - Land of the Dinosaurs. First appearing at the 1964 / 1965 New York World's Fair, before being moved to Disneyland on July 1, 1966, this prehistoric attraction features a world of dinosaurs brought to life through the technology of Audio-Animatronics. A towering Tyrannosaurus Rex battles a Stegosaurus, while a set of Triceratops watch over their new hatchlings and three baby Brontosaurus, affectionately named Huey, Dewey and Louie, make their way about under the watchful eye of a Pterodactyl.

CHAPTER SEVEN

SECRETS OF MICKEY'S TOONTOWN

ROGER RABBIT'S
CAR TOON SPIN

    Disney Imagineers hide secrets which reflect many things. Sometimes it's a bit of Disney history, sometimes it's an homage to a notable Disney figure, and sometimes it's just plain whimsy. As you pass through the queue for Roger Rabbit's Car Toon Spin, look for the ToonTown license plates on the wall. Can you decipher each plate? Here are a few to work on...

CAP 10 HK
FAN TC
101 DLMN
ZPD2DA
IM L8
1D N PTR
L MERM8
RS2CAT
2N TOWN
1DRLND

A Hidden Dalmation

Here's a Disneyland secret for kids of all ages, which usually goes unnoticed because of the placement of the secret. At the entrance to the Toontown Fire Department, there is a doorbell shaped like a small fire hydrant next to the door. Press the red button on the hydrant and then step out and watch the middle window up above. There, one of the puppies from the classic 1961 Disney film *101 Dalmatians* will appear briefly before disappearing again.

Did you notice the address of the fire department, as indicated on the two glass globes out front? How about the year indicated on the shield atop the front of the building? 1928 is appropriate for Toontown! Do you agree the spots on the Dalmatian puppy's head form a Hidden Mickey?

A Hidden Tribute

Throughout Disneyland, there are small tributes to the Imagineers and Cast Members who played an important role in The Walt Disney Company...the windows on Main Street, U.S.A., Fess Parker's window in Frontierland, and the logo for Big Thunder Mountain Railroad are just a few. In Toontown, this same recognition occurs, but for animated characters instead of real people.

Make your way to the Camera Shop and study the nearby windows. Here, just as with Main Street, U.S.A., you will see fictional businesses run by animated characters both famous and obscure, including Jiminy Cricket, The Three Little Pigs and B. B. Wolf (Retired). Outdoor Tours Inc. is run by J. Audubon Woodlore, Park Ranger for Brownstone National Park in a number of Disney animated cartoons from the early to mid-1950s, as well as his large and opportunistic antagonist, Humphrey the Bear.

A HIDDEN MICKEY

As you make the first bend in the queue for Gadget's Go Coaster, study the painted stones in the wall to find a classic Hidden Mickey.

BE THE FIRST IN LINE

This next secret is all in the timing, as well as being "in the know" about what's going on.

Periodically, the "Clockenspiel" above City Hall in Toontown springs to life. Trumpets sound, whistles blow and bells ring as the area comes alive. When you hear this, make your way to City Hall as Disney characters are about to emerge to visit with guests young and old!

WALT DISNEY'S WINDOW

While Disney Imagineers, Cast Members, Disney executives and others are honored with highly visible windows in Disneyland's Town Square, Main Street, U.S.A. and elsewhere, Walt Disney is honored with a set of two small windows atop the Library in Mickey's Toontown.

Wander over to the Library and study the windows up above and to the right. There you'll see two windows in honor of Walt Disney and Laugh-O-Grams Studio, one of the first companies Walt Disney started, and the one which gave him a small taste of all that was to come. Of course, it's fitting that Walt Disney's window is found in the hometown of his partner and friend, Mickey Mouse.

CHAPTER EIGHT

SECRETS OF FANTASYLAND

"What youngster...has not dreamed of flying with Peter Pan over moonlit London, or tumbling into Alice's nonsensical Wonderland? In Fantasyland, these classic stories of everyone's youth have become realities for youngsters of all ages to participate in."

- Walt Disney

A BACKWARDS SLEEPING BEAUTY CASTLE?

Here's a secret with a bit of a twist...or shall we say "turn"?

Disney Legend and Imagineer Herb Ryman designed Disneyland's icon, Sleeping Beauty Castle, using the classic elements of beautiful Neuschwanstein Castle in Bavaria, Germany as his inspiration, and as with all story elements within Disneyland, Herb's concept for the castle was soon turned into a 3-D model so the Imagineers could get a better sense of how it would look once completed. After getting a look at it in 3-D, however, Herb felt something wasn't quite right. According to Herb Ryman...

"One thing that he (Walt) insisted upon was that there be a very, very conspicuous castle, because the castle is going to be the symbol of this whole place. Fred Joerger had done a beautiful model of this castle. When I saw it I said, 'I don't like it.' So I took a look at the castle model, grabbed a hold of the upper portion of the model, and turned it around so that the back of the upper portion now faced the front. 'Dick said, 'Now, Herbie, quit playing with it. Put it back. He said 'Walt's going to be here any minute, and Walt won't like it. Turn it around. Put it back.'"

The next thing you know, Walt walked in. Herb hadn't had a chance to turn the castle back around, so everyone was concerned Walt would be upset with the new look. To the contrary, however. He thought it looked great.

"Walt said, 'Oh, I like that a lot better.' So then Marvin and Dick began to like it a lot better. It was always a confused point with us, but today (the front) is facing inside."

So the front of Sleeping Beauty Castle you see today was originally supposed to be the back!

Take a look at the castle model below, created in 1953 by Marvin Davis and Fred Joerger before Sleeping Beauty Castle was constructed, and see how the appearance of the front of the model more closely resembles the back of the Sleeping Beauty Castle you see in the park today.

1953 Model by Marvin Davis and Fred Joerger

Back of Sleeping Beauty Castle Today

SLEEPING BEAUTY CASTLE WEENIE

In every Disney theme park you'll find a visual "weenie", a dominant park icon which draws guests further into the park. For Disneyland, Sleeping Beauty Castle beckons guests down Main Street, U.S.A. for a day of magic and memories. For the Magic Kingdom, it's Cinderella Castle, for Epcot it's Spaceship Earth and for Disney's Animal Kingdom, it's the Tree of Life.

Using a visual "weenie" to draw in guests was a concept adopted by Walt...

"What you need is a weenie, which says to people 'come this way.' People won't go down a long corridor unless there's something promising at the end. You have to have something that beckons them to 'walk this way.'" – Walt Disney

As Walt designed and built Disneyland, many of the ideas he implemented in his new park were inspired by events from his past; a small mechanical bird discovered in an antique shop in New Orleans provided the inspiration for what would become Audio-Animatronics and Walt Disney's Enchanted Tiki Room, while Marceline, Missouri was the inspiration for Main Street, U.S.A., and of course, a Merry-Go-Round at Griffith Park was the inspiration for Disneyland itself. Walt was always absorbing inspiration throughout his life. There is a story about Walt getting the idea for weenies from when his dog would follow him around whenever he had hot dogs or baloney in his coat pocket, but this strikes me as a bit mundane for a man of Walt's genius. Perhaps...just perhaps...Walt's inspiration for his theme park weenies came from one of the many inspirations he is known to have drawn from his trips to France, including one to Paris in June of 1949.

In 1853, Napolean III directed Georges Eugene Haussmann to reconstruct much of Paris by demolishing its dark and cramped housing along narrow winding streets and replace it with wide boulevards, avenues and open spaces which would let in both sunlight and air. As part of this charge, Haussmann constructed inviting boulevards to connect the different parts of the city, many of which he purposely aligned so that a grand monument, such as the Pantheon, Arc de Triomphe or Opera Palais Garnier, would provide a focal point in the distance. During his lifetime, Walt made a number of trips to Paris, including during his service with the Red Cross as an ambulance driver in 1918, as well as while on a family vacation during 1949, and perhaps it was during one of these visits that Walt drew inspiration from Haussman's open-flowing boulevards with grand focal points for use with his upcoming park, Disneyland.

The Disney Coat of Arms

As you make your way across the drawbridge, and just before you step under the heavy metal portcullis, look up to find the Disney family Coat of Arms. The crest of the coat of arms is composed of three lions passant in pale (arranged vertically, with their right forepaws raised). It was placed there sometime between June of 1964 and July of 1965.

40th Anniversary Time "Castle"

More than just a dramatic icon, Walt Disney designed Sleeping Beauty Castle to draw guests' attention, invite them into the park and act as a central beacon so they wouldn't get lost. However, if you allow the castle to draw your eye to its high turrets and keeps, you'll overlook the 40th Anniversary Time "Castle"...on the ground.

Buried beneath the castle forecourt, just before the drawbridge, is "The Disneyland 40th Anniversary Time Castle." Filled with items from the Disneyland 40th Anniversary

Celebration, its bronze plaque reads...

"Placed beneath this marker on July 17, 1995:

The Disneyland 40th Anniversary Time Castle

A "Time Castle" containing Disneyland memories, messages and milestones, lies beneath this spot. The Disneyland Time Castle is dedicated to the children of the 21st century, who may unlock its contents on the 80th Anniversary of Disneyland, July 17, 2035."

THE CENTER OF DISNEYLAND?

Passing through Sleeping Beauty Castle from the Central Plaza, you will notice a small "golden marker" on the ground near the back portico, immediately below the beautiful hanging clock. It is widely rumored that this marker marks the very center of Disneyland. However, according to Dave Smith, Archives Director for The Walt Disney Company and author of the 760 page "Disney A to Z, The Official Encyclopedia", this marker is not the center of Disneyland and never has been. Nor is it to mark the center of Main Street, U.S.A. In fact, he states that there is no consensus among Disney Imagineers as to the purpose of this small bronze marker or plug. That said, if you ask a Cast Member about it, you're likely to get an answer indicating it's the center of Disneyland...thus the rumor continues.

Point Zero – Paris, France

Note: Because there is no consensus among Disney Imagineers as to the purpose of the bronze marker at Sleeping Beauty Castle, as well as no known reason for it within The Walt Disney Company or elsewhere, I offer up the idea below, *which is purely a supposition on my part.*

In 1949, Walt and his family visited Paris, France, and it is probably safe to say they made sure to visit the stunning gothic cathedral, Notre Dame. In the front plaza of the cathedral, embedded into the stone pavers in a manner similar to the bronze marker at Sleeping Beauty Castle, is the bronze "Point Zero" marker. This small marker is the official center of Paris, as well as the exact point from which all distances throughout France are measured. Could Walt have stood at this marker and taken inspiration from it for the castle he was planning to build in Disneyland only a handful of years later?

Snow White's Grotto

Now exit the backside of Sleeping Beauty Castle and take the pathway immediately to your right to find Snow White's Grotto. For many guests, Snow White's Grotto and the nearby Snow White's Wishing Well are known as the most popular place in Disneyland for marriage proposals. This next secret has to do with a generous gift which presented a Disney Imagineer with a bit of a small problem.

Residing about a waterfall in Snow White's Grotto are eight white statues of Snow White and the Seven Dwarfs. Hand-carved from Carrara marble in Milan, Italy, these were given to Walt in 1958 as a gift from Italian sculptor Leonida Parma. Walt was so impressed by the work that he asked Disney Imagineer John Hench to find a place for them in his new Disneyland park. Unfortunately, this presented John with a problem...Snow White was barely taller than the seven dwarfs, so if placed all together, she would obviously be out of proportion. To solve this, he cleverly turned to "forced perspective" and placed Snow White at the very top of the waterfall, while the Seven Dwarfs were placed down below and slightly closer to guests.

Snow White's Scary Adventures

So many Disneyland Secrets are missed by guests in a hurry, and these next two secrets are no exception. Now visit Snow White's Scary Adventures and look up to the large window above the attraction. Wait for just a moment and you'll see the curtains part to reveal a quick glimpse of the Evil Queen before closing again.

A Shiny Secret

Now step into the queue and find the bronze book and shiny apple at the entrance. While other guests pass by without a clue, take a moment to reach out and touch the apple. Once you do, you'll hear a loud clap of thunder and the menacing cackle of the evil witch.

A Dark Ride Challenge

As you glide, spin or career your way through any of Disneyland's classic "dark rides", the story elements illuminated in black light pop with vivid color, adding a dramatic sense to each story. It's one of the key elements which make them such beloved and classic attractions. Have you ever wondered about the process the Disney Imagineers use to paint these unique black-lit scenes and the challenges they face in doing so? 30 year Imagineer Cindy Bothner explains what's involved...

"Black light painting is a very different animal, because you are basically painting with light. Depending on the amount of regular acrylic paint you mix in with the black colors, you can get a wide variety of light effects. You have to learn to control the amount of black light pigment you use so that everything does not end up popping at the same time. We wanted to avoid giving it the look of a carnival ride. We had to learn to mix our paints so that the piece we were painting looked the same under white light as it did under black light, only with a little more pop to it.

It was very challenging at first. An individual scene was constructed and black dubetyne was put up as a tent. We would paint it under black light in there. Once the scene was finished, a buy-off was scheduled and it was either approved or required changes were made."

King Arthur Carrousel

Now make your way to the King Arthur Carrousel and take a moment to realize the attraction you're enjoying is the oldest in all of Disneyland Resort, with 68 ornately carved horses hand-crafted by artisans in Germany over 100 years ago.

It was a beautiful carrousel which lead to all that is Disneyland today. Walt had taken his two daughters, Sharon and Diane, to ride a carrousel at Griffith Park, and it was here, while sitting on a park bench watching his daughters ride by themselves, that he thought there should be a place where parents could enjoy all of the fun alongside their children. And at that moment the idea of Disneyland was born!

Of course, Walt wanted a carrousel in his new Disneyland, and in 1954 he purchased an 1875 Dentzel Menagerie Carrousel from the Sunnyside Amusement Park in Toronto, Ontario and brought it to California where it was extensively refurbished for guests to enjoy.

A Tribute to a Disney Ambassador and Legend

If you study the horses on the King Arthur Carrousel, you'll find "Jingles", the lead carrousel horse. Adorned with golden bells, Jingles is an honorary tribute to Julie Andrews, who played the title role in Disney's 1964 film "Mary Poppins". Look closely and you'll see this brightly adorned hand-painted horse is themed with icons from the movie, as well as Julie Andrews' initials and bright colorful flowers, which represent her love of gardening.

Flying Over 1955

With the recent re-imagineering of Peter Pan's Flight, the attraction tells even more of the story. Tinker Bell now joins you on your journey, while moonlit London Town is now busy with activity below and Peter Pan challenges Hook in a more engaging battle. However, not everything is brand new, as the Disney Imagineers made sure to keep two story elements, which go all the way back to opening day in 1955. The first is Nana, the Darling's caring dog, who can be seen sitting in the nursery just as you enter the attraction, and the second is the statue of Admiral Nelson, with his sword at his side in London Town.

Mickey's On Board

If you take a moment to ride the nearby Casey Jr. Circus Train attraction, notice the classic three-circle Hidden Mickey in the cab of the train engine as it pulls into the station. Do you see it in the gauges and dials?

My thanks to Disneyland cast member, A. J. Bautista, for pointing this out.

WHO-ARE-U?

Now step into the nearby Mad Hatter shop in Fantasyland for a Disneyland secret which comes and goes. Watch the mirror up on the wall behind the cash register. Do you see him? He's very faint and appears only briefly, but he's there, grinnin' like the Cheshire Cat!

MISSED IN THE BLINK OF AN EYE

Outside and across the way, in the Storybook Land Canal Boats, is Monstro, "a whale of a whale", who swallowed whole Geppetto, Figaro and Cleo in Disney's 1940 animated film, Pinocchio. Most guests simply walk past Monstro without giving him so much as a glance, but if you pause for a moment, you'll find he not only blinks his eye, but also periodically spouts water from his blowhole.

"IT'S A SMALL WORLD"

Now make your way towards "it's a small world", where timing is everything with this next secret. Be in the wrong place at the wrong time, and you're sure to miss it. On the quarter hour, each hour, the clock tower of the "it's a small world" façade opens to reveal a large clock accompanied by small animated dolls which emerge in an entertaining yet brief ceremony.

DISNEYLAND WASN'T
ITS ORIGINAL HOME

Steeped in Disneyland history, "it's a small world" is often assumed to have been a 1955 opening day attraction, but it actually would not appear in the park until nearly 11 years later. Walt Disney and WED Enterprises developed "it's a small world" for the 1964 / 1965 New York World's Fair, where over 10 million visitors from around the world experienced its message of peace and unity. Raising millions of dollars for UNICEF, it was one of the most popular attractions at the fair. After the fair closed, it was then moved to Disneyland and opened to guests on May 28, 1966.

THE MATTERHORN

Opened in 1959, the Matterhorn was born of a trip Walt Disney made to Switzerland in the early 1950s to film "Third Man on the Mountain." Walt was so impressed with the grandeur of the actual Matterhorn in the Alps that he decided he wanted to include it as a main attraction in his plans for Disneyland. The result was the cutting-edge Matterhorn Bobsleds, a thrilling high-speed ride through the upper reaches of the snowy Matterhorn on the very first tubular steel roller-coaster in the world.

AN ABOMINABLE COLLECTION

As you journey deep into the Matterhorn on the Matterhorn Bobsleds, you'll quickly pass by a frozen pile of Disneyland history. Here the Disney Imagineers have built a story around the Abominable Snowman's penchant for collecting colorful and shiny objects, all while giving a nod to the attraction's history, clear back to its opening day in 1959. Observant riders will notice not only old skis, ski poles, lanterns, alpenhorns and other items used by those who traverse the Matterhorn's steep slopes, but also previous Matterhorn Bobsleds ride vehicles and two versions of the colorful sky gondolas, round and rectangular, from the Skyway attraction, which used to pass high above Disneyland and directly through the Matterhorn prior to its closure in 1994.

AN ELUSIVE SECRET

This next secret is as mysterious as the item itself. Make your way near The Matterhorn and search for a cast of the elusive Yeti's large footprint atop a small pedestal. Some claim to have seen it on the north side of the mountain, opposite the boarding area, and others claim to have spotted it on the south side, while countless others who have often visited the mountain claim to have never seen it at all. Find the cast and you will also find a plaque beneath which reads...

Cast of Footprint
Discovered by Matterhorn Expedition
South Slope
May 27, 1978

A True Urban Myth

Matterhorn Bobsleds Poster Art
Signed by Bob Gurr
Author's Personal Collection

Here's a secret which is perhaps one of the strangest in all of Disneyland. Believe it or not, but Cast Members can play basketball *inside* the Matterhorn! The rumor is there's a full-sized basketball court inside, but this isn't true. It's a very small half-court area with a backboard and rim attached to the side of some stairs, all located within a storage area. According to Walt Disney Imagineer Tony Baxter... *"Walt Disney thought, 'What would be the strangest thing to put up there.' And he talked to the people who were both the mountain climbers and the ride operators and asked, 'What would you like to use that space for?', because it was a big empty space up above where the roller coaster ride runs around from about two-thirds on down, but that upper third, the pointed part, was empty. And so they put their heads together and said, 'You know, we like to play basketball.'"* So Walt had a backboard and hoop installed, and it's there to this day as part of Disneyland lore.

A Tribute to an Early Inspiration for Walt Disney

Located in Pixie Hollow is a large (4') jar of "Gertie's Liquid Glue", produced by McCay's Cement Company. More than just a prop, this is an homage to Winsor McCay, a pioneering American cartoonist who played a important role in inspiring a young Walt Disney to become an animator. On February 18th, 1914, when Walt Disney was only 12 years old, Mr. McCay released an innovative silent cartoon titled, "Gertie the Dinosaur", which is widely believed to be one of the very first animated films ever produced.

A Revered Story Element

This next secret, while in plain site, is revealed by the Imagineers to only those who know their Disney history.

Make your way over to the Fairy Tale Treasures gift shop in Fantasy Faire and you'll find Figaro, the cat belonging to Geppetto the woodcarver, who created Pinocchio in Disney's 1940 animated film by the same name. Lying high on an outdoor windowsill, Figaro attempts to take a catnap, but a small bird perched in a cage next to him keeps him awake with its cheerful chirping. This Audio-Animatronic story element in itself is interesting, but the

Imagineers' secret here is that the bird and the cage design are a nod to the small mechanical bird in a cage which Walt discovered in an antique shop in New Orleans. This antique is revered in Disney history, as it inspired Walt to invent Audio-Animatronics, leading to the birds of the Enchanted Tiki Room, President Lincoln and countless other moving figures at Disney theme parks around the world. Of note is the small bird. While not looking anything like the feathered mechanical bird Walt found, the Imagineers programmed this modern day bird with the very same motions as the antique bird, with a swivel of its head, a chirp from its beak and an occasional twitch of its tail feathers. – *Photo courtesy of wwwDisneyGeek.com*

A MYSTERY IN TIME

We finish our tour of the hidden secrets and stories of Disneyland with a mystery.

Suspended by chains in the rear portico of Sleeping Beauty Castle is an ornate chandelier clock installed by Disney Imagineers during a 1996 refurbishment. With no clockworks on the back of the clock face, it seems to always display a time of 4:01. Many guests have assumed it displays the time of Walt's passing, but this is incorrect, as Walt Disney passed away at 9:30 a.m. on December 15, 1966. It also does not display the time of his opening day speech at Disneyland. Can you solve this mystery in time?

THE HIDDEN SECRETS
& STORIES OF
WALT DISNEY WORLD

If you enjoyed discovering the secrets of Disneyland, then you're sure to enjoy *The Hidden Secrets & Stories of Walt Disney World*. The companion book to *The Hidden Secrets & Stories of Disneyland*, it is an entertaining and magical in-depth look at the secret story elements the Disney Imagineers have purposely hidden throughout Walt Disney World...all arranged as a fun tour, complete with photos!

Through countless park visits, interviews, and untold hours of in-depth research, *The Hidden Secrets & Stories of Walt Disney World* presents over 300 fun, whimsical, and fascinating secrets, including never-before-published stories and photos. Available online. Learn more at:

www.Disney-Secrets.com

ACKNOWLEDGMENTS

Many people have graciously contributed to the development of this book. From Michael Broggie's biography of his father and Disney Legend, Roger Broggie, and Jeff Baham's exclusive story about the attic scene in Disneyland's Haunted Mansion, to the Disney Archive's providing a key date for solving a puzzling timeline, and Dave Drumheller's big help in obtaining last-minute photos, many have played a role, large or small, in helping me write a title which contains not only quality content, but also family value entertainment which is respectful of the legacy of Walt Disney.

For that, I would like to thank you all...

- Beth Green - ADisneyMom'sThoughts.com
- Bob Gurr - Disney Legend and Imagineer
- Brian Hillman - George H. Lloyd Relative
- Brian & Meghan Westby - Research Technicians
- Carrie Hayward - DisneyTravelBabble.com
- Chip Confer - ChipandCo.com
- Cindy Bothner - Walt Disney Imagineering
- Dave DeCaro - Davelandweb.com
- Dave Drumheller - WDWGuidedTours.com
- David Lesjak - Disney Historian and Author
- Disneyana Fan Club - Cascade Chapter
- Doug Leonard - Walt Disney Imagineering
- Frank Reifsnyder - Walt Disney Imagineering
- George Eldridge - Decoding the Disneyland Telegraph
- Glenn Barker - Walt Disney Imagineering
- Jack Ferencin - Hellertown, PA
- Jeff Baham - DoomBuggies.com
- Jeff Kober - PerformanceJourneys.com
- Jenn Lissak - DisneyBabiesBlog.com
- Jim Korkis - Disney Historian
- Jason Dziegielewski- DisneyGeek.com
- Jordan Sallis - George H. Lloyd Relative
- Kristy Westby - Research Technician
- Megan Westby - Disneyland Photographer
- Michael & Sharon Broggie - Disney Historians and Authors
- Michael Campbell - President, Carolwood Pacific Historical Society
- Mike Ellis - MyDreamsofDisney.com

- Mike Westby – Disney App and Guidebook Author
- Mousestalgia.com Podcast
- Steve DeGaetano – Disneyland Railroad Historian - SteamPassages.com
- Tammy Benson – Golden Spike NHS
- The Disney Archives

And most of all my parents, Richard & Roberta, for taking me to Disneyland for the very first time many years ago!

SELECTED BIBLIOGRAPHY

Many sources of content, including interviews, books, articles, documents, vintage publications, photos, correspondence, video and of course countless theme park visits were used in the research for this book.

Here are some publications which were not only helpful, but I would highly recommend them as reading material for anyone interested in Disneyland, Walt Disney World or Disney history...

Alexander Brydie, Capt. *A Handbook for Light Artillery.* 1898

Baham, Jeff. *The Unauthorized Story of Walt Disney's Haunted Mansion.* Theme Park Press, 2014

Bain, David Haward. *Empire Express: Building the First Transcontinental Railroad.* Penguin Books, 2000

Berg, Walter G. *Buildings and Structures of American Railroads.* 1893

Broggie, Michael. *Walt Disney's Railroad Story.* Donning Company Publishers, 4th Edition. 2014

DeGaetano, Steve. *The Disneyland Railroad – A Complete History in Words and Pictures.* 1st Edition. 2015

Gabler, Neal. *Walt Disney: The Triumph of the American Imagination.* Alfred A. Knopf, 2006

Kober, J. Jeff. *Disneyland at Work.* Performance Journeys, 2010

Kober, J. Jeff. *Disney's Hollywood Studios – From Show Biz to Your Biz.* Theme Park Press, 2014

Korkis, Jim. The Valult of Walt – Volume 2. Theme Park Press,

2013

Lloyd, George. *George H. Lloyd's Hand Carved Caenstone Model of Our National Capitol.* Lowenstein's, Approx. 1943

Sklar, Marty. *Dream It! Do It!: My Half-Century Creating Disney's Magic Kingdoms.* Disney Editions, 2013

Smith, Dave. *Disney A to Z: The Updated Official Encyclopedia.* Disney Editions, 1998

Strodder, Chris. *The Disneyland Encyclopedia.* Santa Monica Press, 2012

Thomas, Bob. *Walt Disney: An American Original.* Hyperion, 1994

Van Eaton, Mike. *Van Eaton Galleries Presents the story of Disneyland - an exhibition and sale catalog.* 2015

Wright, Alex and The Imagineers: *The Imagineering Field Guide to Disneyland.* Disney Editions, 2008

Wright, Alex and The Imagineers: *The Imagineering Field Guide to Epcot.* Disney Editions, 2006

Wright, Alex and The Imagineers. *The Imagineering Field Guide to The Magic Kingdom.* Disney Editions, 2005

CPSIA information can be obtained
at www.ICGtesting.com
Printed in the USA
FSHW020501220319
56586FS